MW00744495

The Compliance Revolution

The Wiley Finance series contains books written specifically for finance and investment professionals as well as sophisticated individual investors and their financial advisors. Book topics range from portfolio management to e-commerce, risk management, financial engineering, valuation, and financial instrument analysis, as well as much more. For a list of available titles, visit our Web site at www.WileyFinance.com.

Founded in 1807, John Wiley & Sons is the oldest independent publishing company in the United States. With offices in North America, Europe, Australia, and Asia, Wiley is globally committed to developing and marketing print and electronic products and services for our customers' professional and personal knowledge and understanding.

The Compliance Revolution

How Compliance Needs to Change to Survive

DAVID JACKMAN

WILEY

Copyright © 2015 by John Wiley & Sons Singapore Pte. Ltd.

Published by John Wiley & Sons Singapore Pte. Ltd.
1 Fusionopolis Walk, #07-01, Solaris South Tower, Singapore 138628

Other Wiley Editorial Offices
John Wiley & Sons, 111 River Street, Hoboken, NJ 07030, USA
John Wiley & Sons, The Atrium, Southern Gate, Chichester, West Sussex, P019 8SQ, United Kingdom
John Wiley& Sons (Canada) Ltd., 5353 Dundas Street West, Suite 400, Toronto, Ontario, M9B 6HB, Canada
John Wiley& Sons Australia Ltd., 42 McDougall Street, Milton, Queensland 4064, Australia
Wiley-VCH, Boschstrasse 12, D-69469 Weinheim, Germany

Library of Congress Cataloging-in-Publication Data is available

ISBN 9781119020592 (Hardcover)
ISBN 9781119020608 (ePDF)
ISBN 9781119020615 (ePub)

Cover image: birch tree forest ©fet/Shutterstock
Cover design: Wiley

Typeset in 10/12pt, SabonLTStd by SPi Global, Chennai, India.

Printed in Singapore by C.O.S Printers Pte Ltd

10 9 8 7 6 5 4 3 2 1

To my family

Contents

PART THREE
Purpose

Preface

This book is about maturity—*corporate maturity*—how businesses grow up and become more reasoned and responsible, and also more effective and better performing. It is also about the maturing of compliance into a profession, a critical function that sits at the interface between business and wider society. The quest is relevant to all forms of business and to many functions and the models presented here have general applicability.

What maturity is and how to grow is subtle and complex. We contend that however you define or try to create maturity, it is recognizable to customers, employees, and investors—and to regulators, who are increasingly concerned with corporate culture, integrity, governance, and conduct risk.

We use as our example *financial services*, a sector whose responsibility has been much challenged of late and where regulatory approaches and compliance practices are changing apace. Financial services also impacts many other areas of business that are dependent on its role while, as we have seen since the 2008 global financial crisis, its influence spreads out into the wider economy of Main Street and influences the opportunities and prosperity of many across our communities. Compliance has a key position, mediating between the powerful drivers in a highly competitive, complex, and internationalizing industry and the needs of the encircling realm of its multiple stakeholders. We will consider how compliance can use its pivotal role in strategically directing companies towards a more mature and responsible culture. In doing so, the function also transforms itself and demonstrates considerable value.

The rate of change in regulation and compliance has hastened in recent years, partly reflecting the rapid development within the financial services industry and partly because of an internal momentum within regulation that seeks new methodologies and procedures in pursuit of the long-term goal of greater effectiveness and efficiency. This internal momentum generates layer-upon-layer of regulatory reform and consequent compliance evolution, but the processes underlying change have reached such a pitch that recent stages can only be described as requiring a "compliance revolution." This revolution is just starting, and the most significant steps are still to come.

However, few in compliance, regulation, or senior management are aware of this revolution, its implications for the wider business, and how compliance needs to prepare and lead. A primary purpose of this book is to make compliance practitioners aware of this revolution, how to manage change, and what is required of them. If compliance fails to step up, it is likely that the function will lose influence and become marginalized. The opportunity for professionalizing may not return.

Part of the armory of any profession is a clear model and narrative of how it adds value to businesses and the wider economy. This is absent for compliance, which has been historically reactive, subject to fashion, and somewhat cyclical. Here we attempt to fulfill the urgent need for an overall development model for compliance and regulation. We also add a new suite of technologies and methodologies that give more meat to its practices and buttress a claim for professionalism.

The book comprises three parts:

Part I: Theory—a model of regulatory and compliance development

Part II: Practice—tools and techniques to improve compliance performance

Part III: Purpose—the overall aims and drivers of new compliance

Compliance is at a fork in the road. If compliance steps up its value, its status will be enhanced; miss the opportunity, and other functions may well appropriate traditional territory. This book aims to help compliance, regulators, and businesses make wiser, more mature choices.

David Jackman
Easedale
2015

Acknowledgments

The concepts and tools here are the product of a long and almost continual internal conversation, informed by endless field testing on firms, sectors, and industries in different jurisdictions. The thesis does not draw heavily on any existing body of work or adopt a particular philosophic position, but picks, jackdaw-like, from a wide selection of relevant sources and examples—we hope constructed to form an elegant whole.

Many say ethics and compliance are important but few wish to think very deeply, and would rather be told. This is, of course, part of the problem we address. Some elements are pioneering and ahead of their time but many are now, pleasingly, embedded in the mainstream. This book weaves these threads together and provides an opportunity to look into the distance once again.

Places have been more yielding. Much of this text has been composed during wanderings in Easedale, which the poet Thomas de Quincy correctly called "paradise in miniature." Inspiration has also come from Edinburgh, Singapore, Dublin, Sligo, and Shrewsbury.

I am grateful for the support of Geoffrey Rowell, Howard Davies, Phillip Thorpe, Sue Proudfoot, Cameron Butland, British Standards (BSi), PayPlan Ltd., Patricia Lee, and many classes of students.

Finally, I am indebted to Alexander for his incisive editing, and my wife, who is better qualified in these areas than most of us.

About the Author

David Jackman, MA, PGCE, FRSA, had an Exhibition to Oxford and a double distinction from Cambridge, as well as experience in an executive-tier bank management scheme and in teaching, before entering regulation in 1990. He co-founded the Securities Institute (now the Chartered Institute for Securities and Investments) and developed an agenda of prevention, education, and ethics applied at IMRO and during the formation of the UK's Financial Services Authority (FSA).

On Halloween 2002, David launched "An Ethical Framework for Financial Services"—the first ethical statement published by a financial regulator. The concepts in FSA Discussion Paper 18 now underpin approaches to regulation in many jurisdictions.

Following a chief executive role for the Financial Services Skills Council, and then visiting professor for the London Financial Academy, *The Ethical Space* was formed to work on this broad agenda with boards and organisations from all sectors. David has non-executive directorships and lectures and commentates on the BBC and in the press and researches. He has a long association with the regulator-supported Singapore ICTA diplomas and master classes in Kuala Lumpur.

As primary author of the UK National Standards for Sustainable Development (BS8900) and Sustainable Communities (BS8904), David also leads the UK's contribution to groundbreaking international standards for sustainable communities and smart cities. He has founded a Community Interest Company, the 21st Century Charter, the World Open Forum, the Ethics Mark, and the Ethics Foundation.

A portal is offered in support of this book: www.intotheclearing.com.

Theory

The landscape of regulation and compliance is changing fundamentally. New elements are emerging that bring new sets of priorities, approaches, and methodologies. Chapter 1 shows how compliance needs to move in a more strategic direction.

To understand this change in direction, we need a map. A theoretical model is set out in Chapter 2 giving a coherent picture of the past and future development of regulation and compliance. This is our base map for understanding the past and future development of regulation and compliance. This framework also helps to explain why change happens, and what regulation and compliance should do to be properly prepared and fully engaged.

The model is based on financial services but could be applied to any industry or sector. While we primarily use examples from the UK and Singapore, which are both leading the way in their respective spheres, similar patterns can be found around the world. Not all jurisdictions are travelling at the same rate, so the model can be used to classify them and predict their future path.

Chapter 3 reminds us that the record of compliance over the last decade has been difficult. This is partly because the changes underway prior to the Global Financial Crisis (GFC) of 2008 were not properly embedded by the time they were severely tested. This demonstrates clearly those firms and compliance practitioners who fail to understand the Bigger Picture and embed change are running a significant individual and corporate risk.

One

Theory

CHAPTER 1

New Compliance

See the whole among the pieces.
—Cameron Butland and David Jackman, Twenty-First
Century Charter (21CC; June 2, 2009)

THE CHALLENGE

Compliance is undergoing a revolution in underlying principles, practices, role, expectations, and value. But many involved in governance, risk, and compliance (GRC) do not recognise the importance of the changes underway or understand how best to react and lead. This book aims to explain the significance of the phase we are now entering in financial services and provides a guide for compliance practitioners to navigate the transition in a way that is applicable to any sector or jurisdiction.

Compliance is growing rapidly across the world as regulatory requirements become more complex and international. The compliance function is now growing faster than many other roles but in many cases remains operational and mechanical; relative to its level of responsibility and potential impact, compliance is low status and poorly integrated into mainstream business activities. It is often considered an expensive add-on, marginalised, seen as a barrier to successful business, bedeviled by silo mentality and simplistic approaches.

This has to change. Compliance must show itself to be high-value, pivotal, and strategic. To achieve this there needs to be a fundamental shift in:

- How compliance sees itself
- Intellectual capital
- Overall direction and narrative
- Tools and methodologies
- Competences and professionalism

Yet the primary reason for this change is not self-preservation or self-enhancement, but because the aims and deliverables of compliance are so important to so many. The outcomes of compliance are critical to individual customers, families, businesses, and to the interests of the wider economy and society.

TURNING POINT

A turning point has been reached in financial services regulation. This text picks up the story of regulatory and compliance development at this crucial inflection. This is the moment at which compliance comes of age. It is no longer acceptable or credible to hide behind box ticking or "having appropriate systems and controls in place." The differentiator is professional maturity. This is not possible without a focus on corporate and sector-wide maturity.

The journey on which compliance—and regulation—is embarking runs uphill. The path is steep and at times indistinct and difficult. There is a need to develop many tools and resources to assist the climb. However, this book sets out a general direction of travel and equips the reader with as much of the basic equipment as is possible to make a safe and successful ascent.

What is paramount is speed. The journey needs to be embarked upon soon and with urgency. What is undoubtedly true is that the range and complexity of the problems mounting are extraordinary and the need for solutions in an unequal and globalizing world is pressing. Compliance and regulation generally has a valuable role in making or facilitating and, on occasion, leading progress for both firms and the wider community, far beyond its popular image.

TRADITIONAL COMPLIANCE

Traditional compliance, as we shall refer to mechanical practices, is not covered here. There are many texts on introducing risk-based approaches or capital models. Other traditional elements of compliance include basic fitness and properness tests, authorization, client money rules, know your customer, market manipulation rules, transparency requirements, and financial promotions regulations and conduct of business rules. These are all important but they represent the foundation level of regulation and compliance and are not sufficient to constitute a sophisticated control environment or justify compliance as a full profession.

Similarly, fighting financial crime and money laundering have a basic of traditional compliance but have a sufficiently different set of objectives and processes to mark them out as a separate sub-discipline. It is more difficult to apply the models and tools introduced in this book to this parallel stream.

A final traditional tenet to be challenged is that compliance is not synonymous with or part of risk; it is much bigger than that. There may be compliance or regulatory risks within a risk framework but it does not follow from that that compliance is in some way subservient to risk or should be part of the risk department. Compliance, as we shall see in Parts II and III, has a much more strategic and wide-ranging scope and should report to the board independently and directly. Having a compliance person or specific *non-executive director* (NED) on the board is a clear sign that compliance has stepped up and not been left behind.

NEW COMPLIANCE

More than can perhaps be imagined depends on a *new compliance* emerging. This requires regulators and compliance to engage in a shared journey in which both are investing heavily in research, education, and discussion while establishing new joint approaches and infrastructures. We examine these new structures and elements and how they work together for a new compliance in Part II.

SHARED JOURNEY

It is important that the journey to new compliance is a shared one with compliance and regulation following the same map—the map is suggested in Chapter 2.

Ideally, regulation and compliance should be able to move forward in partnership at the same rate, but too often one side is playing catchup. If regulation is ahead of compliance, firms may be subject to increased regulatory risk, and if compliance gets ahead of regulation, then the risk is of unexpected interpretations increasing regulatory firm risk and regulators suffering reputational damage and loss of support by appearing flatfooted.

Regulation's role is to reflect and mediate the expectations and requirements of the wider public and economy. Regulatory objectives are rarely unreasonable, but regulators often lack the practical business experience to know how to implement them effectively and in a balanced way. Conversely, compliance should have the hands-on experience but may be more distant from the policy agenda or democratic public needs. Obviously, a dynamic process of learning from each other is ideal, but this needs a facilitative infrastructure, a basis of trust, and extensive practice. The crucibles for building mutual understanding may be shared training vehicles, informal discussion groups, frequent communication documents, and staff exchange programmes.

The most important shared understanding is that regulation and compliance are not ends in themselves. This self-delusion is dangerous and both compliance practitioners and regulators need to remind each other of their wider role and the implications of their actions. Both needs to have a shared answer to the question: *Why do we do what we do?* We consider that in Part III.

CHAPTER 2

General Model of Regulatory and Compliance Development

It is not the strongest or the most intelligent who will survive but those who can best manage change.

—Charles Darwin

INTRODUCTION TO DEVELOPMENT MODELS

Charles Darwin set out a general model to describe the evolution of species and the principles of competition and natural selection. Adam Smith, similarly, provided a general model of economic development and described the operation of comparative advantage.

So development models usually have two basic components:

1. An overall direction and stages of development
2. Processes underlying change.

Regulation and compliance needs an overall picture of its development, including the major stages in that journey and an explanation of the processes by which change occurs. A general model is proposed here to help explain the pathway of change and to uncover the processes driving development. This in turn gives a clearer view of the future.

The usual caveats about models apply: there are variations in the fine detail, different cultures and jurisdictions develop at different rates, and progress is rarely linear. But models provide an easily comprehended picture that we can then re-complicate, adding all the appropriate variables to apply it to our own situation and circumstances.

Crucially, a model gives us vision, a way of summarising the past and helping us deal with future uncertainties. This is what compliance needs so badly: a narrative about where it has come from, and a map for its future progress and development.

GENERAL MODEL OF REGULATORY AND COMPLIANCE DEVELOPMENT

The model in Figure 2.1 describes a process of maturity. This is the development of regulation and compliance from start-up, through early and "teenage" years, to a more grownup state. This provides a model for understanding and evaluating each stage of a regulatory–compliance system. It also supplies a roadmap for future growth and improvement and may be considered at the levels of a:

- Jurisdiction
- Sector or subsector
- Firm

It is not necessarily the case that all firms operating from or within a jurisdiction will be at the same level of maturity as the jurisdiction as a whole. There will be a range of maturities of individual firms or even subsectors, and this causes interesting problems both for the laggards and for the regulators concerned.

The model identifies five stages. These are clearly not mutually exclusive but blend one into another, each building on the others:

1. *Start-up:* Establishing credibility by using direct, often simple and easy-to-implement measures to combat an obvious and commonly agreed problem. Enforcement at this stage is often punitive, and rule breaches are described in technical terms. Regulation may operate in an apparently business-friendly way, and may be through self-regulatory organisations that are close to the issues and allow governance by peers.

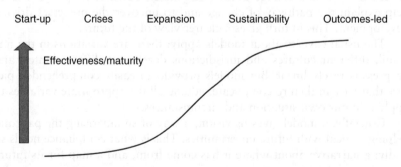

FIGURE 2.1 General Model of Regulatory and Compliance Development

This stage may offer perfectly adequate protection for some societies and be a rational place to remain for some time, but regulators credibility and effectiveness may be undermined when crises emerge.

2. *Crises:* This stage is characterised by reactive and often disorganised or disproportional responses to emergent problems (e.g., 2008 GFC), or the unexpected consequences of earlier interventions (e.g., UK 1980s and 1990s pensions mis-selling). Changes are often driven by public opinion and political necessity that may see extra regulation as the only credible quick fix. This may be the trigger for a secondary wave of reform involving the rationalisation of regulatory and compliance structures. Societies may revert to these crisis conditions at any time in the development path and can cause progress to temporarily retreat down the curve.

3. *Expansion:* Here, regulation becomes more proactive and confident, often associated with clearer objectives (e.g., UK Financial Services and Markets Act 2000), and extensions of scope into more fringe areas (e.g., insurance and mortgages), usually based on the pressing consumer protection expectations of a newly wealthy middle-class. Regulation almost inevitably becomes more expensive, bureaucratic, and unresponsive under the pressure of size, and therefore potentially higher risk. This is compounded by resistance and lack of consensus within the industry, which now seems more distant.

4. *Sustainability:* Recognition that expansion cannot continue exponentially. Regulatory and compliance toolboxes become more fit-for-purpose and sophisticated. Methods of rationalisation and performance improvement now include:

- Risk-focused compliance
- Cost-benefit analysis
- Principles-based regulation
- Emphasis on prevention—focusing on corporate culture (conduct risk), ethics, and governance
  The emphasis here shifts significantly from controlling precisely individual internal process to framing the internal and external environment around a firm or sector in such a way as to increase the likelihood of positive behaviours.

5. *Outcomes-led:* Focus on systemic outcomes on the wider economy and society (and occasionally, environment). By evaluating impacts as part of the regulatory mix, regulation incorporates an understanding of the community purposes of regulation and the effects in social and economic terms that interventions are seeking to create. An outcomes-based system allows for far more creative methods of compliance and regulation where systems and processes is not the ultimate goal. New external criteria bring new criteria for success and enforcement, and allow regulation to be employed for a wider range of objectives.

The Difficult Step—Stage 3 to 4/5

Each stage builds on the last and introduces additional regulatory and compliance tools and priorities. Part II will focus on the new components introduced in stages 4 and 5. In Part III we will see how these stages add the essential components of an infrastructure (we shall call this the *Ethical Space*) necessary to enable compliance to be strategically effective and contribute towards corporate maturity. We will also find in Part III that the processes at work in stages 1–3 reach a critical point when entering stages 4 and 5. This "difficult step" is from stage 3 to 4/5 and requires a *revolution* in commitment and the depth and rate of change.

Limitations of the Model

Any development model has limitations and some of the questions to consider are:

- Is the length of each stage the same, or can stages be elongated or shortened?
- Is it possible to skip a stage entirely and move from one stage to the next without, for example, the stage of crises?
- Is it possible to regress? Is progress irreversible?
- Can you get stuck in one stage? If so, why?
- Is a final downturn inevitable, or will the curve continue upwards?

In some cases crises set the underlying development curve back a stage or two as regulators can often feel more secure and demonstrate credibility by resorting to "tougher," more familiar ways. But this effect is usually short-lived and can be detrimental to restoring confidence because enforcement actions become more visible and numerous and undermine the maturity of the relationship between regulator and industry sector. It is better in the long term for regulators to keep their eye fixed on the development model and to return to the trajectory as soon as possible.

In the specific case of the 2008 financial crisis, the progression to a more sustainable stage had started before the crisis broke. The shift of approach was not dependent on the crisis as a trigger. However, the crisis, while causing a short-term step backwards in the way suggested above, further drove the progression of regulation and set more favourable conditions for both achieving sustainable regulation and also refocusing on outcomes. The foremost lesson for politicians and the public from the 2008 crisis is that "Problems of Wall Street cause problems on Main Street."

INTERNATIONAL COMPARISONS

It is possible to place regulatory regimes or jurisdictions along the development curve in terms of their stage in the journey. Some may be large and powerful regulators in terms of legal powers, reach and style of enforcement action but that does not mean that they are sophisticated in terms of the mix of approaches used. Equally, this does not mean that such regimes are not effective, but they could be more effective if they advanced their methodologies and added to their regulatory toolkit. It is also the contention that compliance will be more embedded and therefore resilient under pressure if regulators move up the development curve. Stages 4 and 5 are inherently lower cost and so more sustainable in the long term.

In general terms many regulatory–compliance systems are not as far along the curve as they need to be given the challenges they face and increasing public expectations. This partly explains why regulation and compliance has been viewed as less-than-fully-effective during and after the 2008 financial crash – as we will explore in Chapter 3. There have also been examples of regulatory failure in other sectors, e.g., phone hacking in the UK media, which gives the impression that regulation in general, is ineffective.

Regulation is a social activity, and the development of one regulatory system tends to drag along others. Some regulators tend to be cautious and do not want to be 'first movers,' while others are more competitive or seek to be the beacon in a particular region or sector. If advancements made by one seem to be successful, it is only a matter of time before other regulators follow. The key to future international success is that there is a critical mass of regulators that pursue the direction towards stages 4 and 5, impressing on those in stages 1–3 the need to move forward. This is particularly important simply to reduce the opportunities for arbitrage between jurisdictions.

To re-emphasise a conclusion from Chapter 1, the primary advantage of the regulation–compliance system progressing along the developmental model curve is that it can deliver more effectively the social/economic outcomes for the wider community. This is the end; compliance and regulation are only means to that end.

EXAMPLE OF THE UK

The UK is a useful example of the development of a financial services regulatory system (see Table 2.1) and has been tracked to a greater or lesser extent by many other jurisdictions, including Singapore.

TABLE 2.1 Examples of the general model of regulatory and compliance development from UK financial services regulation—characteristics from each stage Jackman, D 2015.

Dates (approximate)	Stage	Example
1986–1992	Start-up	Establishment of sectoral self-regulatory organisations (SROs) at deregulation; The Securities Association (TSA), the Life Assurance and Unit Trust Regulatory Organisation (Lautro), the Financial Intermediaries, Managers and Brokers Regulatory Authority (FIMBRA) and the Investment Management Regulatory Organisation (IMRO) overseen by the Securities and Investments Board (SIB). Process rules for fact-finds, transparency, and training and competence. Bank of England supervises large banking institutions.
1992–1998	Crises	Bank of Credit and Commerce International (BCCI), Polly Peck and Mirror Pension Scheme (Maxwell) raised concerns about corporate governance and Bank of England banking oversight. Pensions mis-selling and Equitable Life suggested self-regulators too close to industry.
1998–2007	Expansion	Formation of Financial Services Authority (FSA) under Financial Services and Markets Act (FISMA) 2000, combining 10 prior regulatory bodies, including SROs. Extending depth of regulation (for example, in banking) and scope (e.g., mortgages and general insurance). FSA rulebook expands to 9,500 pages, although supervision increasingly risk based and statutory requirement for cost-benefit analysis (CBA). Increasing consumer focus.
2007–2013	Sustainable	Recognition that regulatory burden is counterproductive, costly, and discouraging location of international businesses in London. Shift to more principles-based regulation (MPBR). Increased emphasis on ethics, culture, and "treating customers fairly" (TCF). Rationale reinforced by 2008 financial services crisis. Focus on high-risk sectors using wider range of regulatory tools and themed reviews and visits. Enforcement action escalates, resulting in higher levels of fines.
2013–future	Outcomes-led	Formation of Financial Conduct Authority (FCA) in 2013 following dissolution of FSA. Bank of England regains systemically significant banking supervision through Prudential Regulatory Authority (PRA). FCA concentrates on culture (conduct risk) and governance issues (e.g., LIBOR fixing, money laundering, data controls). Supervision is more thematic and outcomes led.

USING REGULATORY TOOLKITS

It is the combination of approaches and tools that delivers effective compliance and regulation, not one set replacing the previous set. There exists a growing compliance and regulatory menu or toolkit, but it is how the elements are selected and used together that is the real skill. The range of tools available and the sophistication with which they are combined and used determines the maturity of the jurisdiction and the professionalism of the compliance sector. How the mix is balanced and selected for any one firm or set of circumstances is decided upon and delivered by regulators and compliance officers making critical judgments, not following checklists or risk models only. How good these professional judgments are really matters. Quality judgment is what firms and societies pay for.

To decide how successful a regulator is in using this toolkit, the Monetary Authority of Singapore (MAS), has the following tests or tenets:

- Is the financial system as a whole stable even in the instance of the failure of one or more financial institutions?
- Is the financial system serving the needs of customers and the economy efficiently?
- Are regulatory standards of a high quality, consistent with international standards and best practice, yet appropriate to the local context?
- Is there shared ownership of the desired outcomes of regulation among stakeholders?
- Does the balance of benefits and costs weigh in favour of regulation?
- Are market incentives alone likely to deliver a desired outcome?
- Are the obligations imposed by regulation on regulated entities clear?
- Does regulation take into proper account market practices and legitimate commercial considerations?
- Does regulation provide regulated entities with legal certainty and predictability where it is needed and, where appropriate, flexibility to apply their own practices to meet regulatory objectives?
- Does the regulation provide a level playing field for potentially competing activities and institutions?
- Does regulation recognise that some institutions may have lower risk profiles and stronger governance and controls? Does it provide differentiated treatment where appropriate and can it adjust in a timely fashion if the risk profile changes?
- Is the regulatory framework able to adapt to fast-changing practices and products as well as to new risks in the financial services industry so that it can continue to be effective in respect of its intended regulatory objective and impose obligations that remain appropriate?[1]

CONCLUSION

This chapter provides the framework for the remainder of the book: a model to evaluate differing regulatory systems and a roadmap for the future.

Before we explore stages 4 and 5 in detail, and even suggest a stage 6, we will just reflect on recent experience and the difficulty some leading jurisdictions have had in stepping up from stage 3 to 4/5. Obviously, this transition, which we recognize is the most difficult in conceptual and practical terms, has been made even more difficult by the 2008 GFC. The GFC placed strains on the early steps in this transition as change had not had the chance to become sufficiently embedded. So now these jurisdictions have a chance to make the transition for a second time and ensure that it sticks.

ENDNOTE

1. Monetary Authority of Singapore, *Tenets of Effective Regulation* (revised 2013). Singapore: MAS, p. 9, http://www.mas.gov.sg/~/media/MAS/About%20MAS /Monographs%20and%20information%20papers/Tenets%20of%20Effective %20Regulationrevised%20in%20April%202013.pdf (accessed 13/12/2014).

CHAPTER 3

Is Compliance Worth the Money?

Bolt pulls up the ladder, secures the hatch.
—Simon Armitage, "Last Day on Planet Earth," in *Seeing
Stars* (London: Faber and Faber, 2010)

AN UNFORTUNATE UNCONFORMITY

Compliance has not had a happy record since 2008. This is partly because
the apparent development in compliance and regulation into stage 4 of the
General Model may have been superficial and not properly embedded. Also
other firms and regulators were either complacent or comfortable in stage 3
and had failed to improve. In general, where regulators had been trying to
press forward into stage 4, such as the UK's Treating Customers Fairly (TCF)
initiative, compliance may not have had the frame of reference to have really
got it, and so were unable to keep in step with changing regulatory expectations. This created an unstable unconformity between pioneering regulators
and compliance. This is a high-risk situation for a regulatory and compliance system.

This unconformity may have left compliance looking somewhat
bewildered and embarrassed. Remedial actions have also seemed hasty
and superficial, rather than embedded. So, despite regulation beginning
to enter stages 4 and 5, the compliance results in the same period have
been uncertain and fragile—as 2008 unearthed. It is reasonable to assume
that development in compliance needs to progress further and faster, as
Part II suggests, as some firms start from a position well behind the curve.
Compliance must play catchup. But before setting out in a determined
fashion it is necessary to consider the shortcomings we saw first time
around, and this may help focus on how best to change.

THE 2008 GLOBAL FINANCIAL CRISIS

In 2006, the author wrote an article in the financial press warning that "the emperor has no clothes,"[1] and so it proved. There were many causes of the 2008 GFC. Compliance failings were central. But it is also fair to say that the roots of the crisis and the contributory factors were many and various. The undoubted compliance failings were by no means the only factors adding to international instability. Causes and accelerators were to be found in almost every component of the financial system, including:

- Encouragement of the subprime sector by government policies, starting in the 1990s or even before.
- Target-driven selling in banks.
- Bonus culture.
- Relaxed and competitive credit policies.
- Consumer greed—wants became needs.
- Regulators, governments, and banks were happy to sustain the myth of continuing runaway growth. UK Chancellor Gordon Brown announced that New Labour had "abolished the cycle of boom and bust" as far back as 1997[2]—all seemed delighted to believe him.
- Voters and consumers were comfortable and complacent and therefore unchallenging.
- Inadequacy of capital models and business-as-usual stress-tests.
- Panic due to a lack of understanding of complex products, the real levels of toxicity and liquidity.
- Retail banks trying to behave as though they were investment banks or being led by their investment bank arms (and acquiring such arms if need be, e.g., RBS's takeover of ABN AMRO in the midst of the crisis).
- Lack of product due diligence by buyers of complex products such as *collateralized debt obligations* (CDOs)
- Sometimes knowing connivance amongst the producers of complex products as disclosed by the U.S. Congressional hearings.
- Interconnectedness of the global financial system and some banks discovered to be "too big to fail" (e.g., Lehman Brothers).
- Lack of international cooperation and information sharing until it is was almost too late.

The FSA Turner report highlighted from this list:[3]

- Unsustainable credit boom and asset price inflation (with inadequate capital requirements)
- Increasing complexity and opacity of the securitised credit model

- Misplaced reliance on sophisticated mathematics
- Transmission of loss of confidence and bank funding liquidity into real economy effects
- Hardwired procyclicality creating self-reinforcing feedback loops
- Impaired ability to extend credit to the real economy exacerbating the economic downturn

Economist Robert Shiller added:

> The central bankers didn't see it as their mission to think about mortgages that are being written or to worry about the shadow-banking sector, because they weren't banks so they weren't under supervision, so they let things go. Those are mistakes, but understandable given the bureaucratic structure.[4]

Compliance failing included:

- Insufficient due diligence seems to have been carried out on complex products traded.
- Insufficient attention was paid by compliance on the capital or funding positions of banks.
- Insufficient warnings were given about lending practices such as high multiples of income, low deposit requirements, buy-to-let mortgages, self-certified mortgages, and mortgages over 100 percent of asset value.
- Modelling of stressed situations that could arise was insufficient.
- Aggressive advertising and rewards were obvious but unchecked.
- Some more conservative banks, such as Standard Chartered and HSBC, to an extent, stood aloof, but this did not encourage different patterns of behaviour amongst the compliance community.

These are the basics of compliance supervision. There may be instances where individual compliance officers had insight and spoke up, but they were either not listened to or did not have the stature or import to make a meaningful difference. Some, it is understood, were relieved of their duties for their efforts as the race for new business was on.

Regulators' relative inaction and lack of pressure made it difficult to find an intellectual justification for a more compliance intervention. Particularly inexplicable was the unwillingness of regulators and compliance to do anything very differently after the early warning collapse of Northern Rock in 2007. Unfortunately, the performance of regulators and of compliance are actually and metaphorically bound together.

LEGACY OF FAILURE

Given compliance's recent record, it would be reasonable for boards, governments, and consumers to ask whether compliance is actually worth the money. Why should companies, the industry collectively, or its many stakeholders have confidence in the compliance function?

Yet, despite this record, firms and financial systems across the world continue to plough increased resources into the compliance sector. Compliance is one of the fastest growing functions in the industry. Progressively fewer businesses view regulation as a burden, and while in 2007, prior to the crash, 76 percent of UK businesses surveyed predicted that the "burden from regulation would increase" in the next year, this figure fell to 43 percent.[5]

Why is this, when a rational response would be to cut budgets, numbers, and status and try some other way? Why may businesses be more accepting of regulation following a crisis than in times of plenty? The answer lies in the question. There is no plan B, no other way available, apparently, for the moment. This lack of alternative has allowed an opportunity for compliance and regulators to reassert their credibility. The default setting continues to be more rules, more and heavier enforcement intervention, and more expectations placed on compliance functions. The industry and its stakeholders seem to have no other option but to continue to believe in the compliance infrastructure as the principal instrument for maintaining stability and improving outcomes. However, the legacy of failure includes:

1. Firms parceling out elements of compliance responsibility to neighbouring functions such as risk, legal, and business development, which may be considered more reliable, technical, and professional.
2. Regulators circumventing or mechanizing compliance functions (e.g., FCA Gabriel reporting systems and board attestation).

A recent informal survey of compliance officers carried out in Singapore showed a greater tendency for:

- Heads of compliance to report through a risk function
- Compliance processes switched to risk, legal, and other functions
- The balance of compliance control to be assigned away from central compliance functions to staff embedded in the line who may or may not be answerable or committed to compliance functions or have adequate and transferrable compliance skills
- Compliance to be left with routine processing, although often with larger numbers of staff working in silo roles such as onboarding and KYC (Know Your Customer)

Taken together, these items have the potential in the longer term to demote compliance to a second-rate operational function. Most worrying of all is the denigration of compliance decision-making by increased tick-boxing, data gathering, and system-driven monitoring. This erodes the very capability, self-confidence, and judgment that is essential to compliance's long-term survival and enhanced value.

One of the arguments to prevent further erosion of responsibilities must be that risk and governance functions were equally culpable in the 2008 financial crisis. One of the key findings of the 2009 Walker Report was that:

> Serious deficiencies in prudential oversight and financial regulation in the period before the crisis were accompanied by major governance failures within banks.[6]

POST-2008

The rehabilitation of compliance might be more convincing if compliance's record since 2008 had been better. Much of what is being discovered now is historic, but there are also new cases that relate entirely to the post-2008 period. This is despite changes in bank leadership, new governance standards, and numerous ethical and cultural change programmes.

Recent Issues

1. Rate Fixing One of the systemic failings to emerge from the post-2008 analysis has been the scale of rate fixing across several financial centres, including London, Singapore, Hong Kong, and Shanghai, both during the GFC and afterwards. The revelations show the level of cynical manipulation of the system for the advantage of individual banks, first to disguise vulnerabilities during the 2008 crisis, and later for competitive advantage. The effects across the system are incalculable because so many institutions and consumers have been affected. It seems compliance was again unable or unwilling to identify or address this systematic misuse of a lightly regulated part of the system. It is possible that regulators knew about the possibility of fixing—the leaked emails of Barclay's workers certainly suggest that it was common knowledge among traders—but compliance seemed impotent. In 2014, five banks were fined by FCA for fixing foreign exchange rates:

1. Citibank NA: £225,575,000 ($358 million)
2. HSBC Bank Plc: £216,363,000 ($343 million)
3. JPMorgan Chase Bank NA: £222,166,000 ($352 million)

4. The Royal Bank of Scotland Plc: £217,000,000 ($344 million)
5. UBS AG: £233,814,000 ($371 million)

Barclays chose not to settle with the others but rather decided to seek an integrated settlement.

2. Rogue Traders Despite the additional resources applied to compliance since 2008, rogue traders have emerged at major banks. Some of the most dramatic losses are:

- Société Général: Jerome Kervial managed to evade detection for long enough to amass losses of nearly €5 billion from €38 billion in unauthorised trades. A second round of fines were levied in May 2015. Despite the high fines involved some questioned whether the banks had been treated lightly given the criminal nature of the charges.
- UBS: Kweku Adoboli traded illegally with possibly the knowledge of his colleagues but not compliance for two years and cost the bank over £1.5 billion.
- JP Morgan: Bruno Iksil's "London Whale" trades of 2012 may have lost in excess of $7 billion.

In these and other cases it often seems that other traders and possibly superiors knew of the rogue trades, but not, somehow, compliance.

3. Mis-selling There have been numerous examples of mis-selling such as the overselling of payment protection insurance (PPI) to thousands of customers, which started before 2008 but continued well beyond. The compensation or restitution schemes have cost billions of pounds. The balance of gain and reward with this product turned out to be obviously unfairly tilted towards the banks. A second example is the selling of highly complex foreign exchange products to small businesses that they neither understood nor needed.

Lehman Brothers' Hong Kong and Singapore offices sold small-denomination bonds to retail investors as low-risk investments via distributors. However, they failed to inform investors of the true structure of the product, which included collateralised debt obligations (CDOs). These "minibonds" then collapsed with Lehman's in 2008, dragging down investors. The MAS imposed sales bans on 10 distributing banks, which paid S$104.6 million in compensation.[7]

The growing popularity of crowd sourced financing may be the next source of mis-selling.

4. Governance Failings Governance failings were highlighted in the collapse of Royal Bank of Scotland (RBS), most particularly reflecting the dominance of an iconic chief executive and the triumph of personal ambition over sound judgment. Again compliance was ignored.

A wide range of other cases have emerged such as the UK's Co-operative Bank, where it appears Chair Paul Flowers seemed incapable of leading a large bank and allowed a gap in the finances to open up.

5. Money-Laundering and Data Protection The sanctions busting and money laundering of HSBC has led to a level of fines and recovery work prompting the CEO to become exasperated. But to imagine that compliance could not have reasonably assumed Mexico was high risk in terms of drugs money is inconceivable. That the bank should have had extra compliance controls seems obvious, and its lapses call into question the enormous resources put into play by banks around the world.

Standard Chartered private bank found in December 2013[8] that outsourcing—in particular of customer records—is a highly risky operation and data loss or misuse can lead to large reputational damage.

Cybercrime and identity theft have emerged as a significant operational risk and demand new skill sets of compliance.

6. Tax Evasion In 2015, the Geneva branch of HSBC attracted a storm of media attention and public condemnation over its facilitation of tax evasion for clients. HSBC senior directors had to answer before a UK Parliamentary Select Committee in March 2015. There are likely to be wider repercussions of this trend, as especially U.S. and UK tax authorities seek to recover unpaid tax from their citizens.

7. Retrospective Reviews The retrospective application of new, higher standards to situations where these standards did not apply, or were not specific, is an issue that contributes to the unflattering view of compliance. For example, an FSA thematic review of the self-invested pension plans (SIPPs) sector in September 2009 set new standards of good practice that were not normal practice or formal guidance but could be used to judge business conducted at an earlier time. It raises the point that compliance often needs to be super-equivalent and the effect is to contribute to the basic narrative that compliance standards historically have been too low.

8. Corruption It is interesting to note that corruption is a wider issue being tackled more openly and widely on a number of fronts both inside and outside of financial services. In May 2015, for example, US law enforcement officers started to follow up allegations of corruption in FIFA and across the sport of football relating to sponsorship deals and the awarding of World Cup bids. There have been investigations of corruption in the operation of drug companies selling products in China, Siemens in engineering and in mining, hiding conflict minerals extraction. This raises the consciousness of corruption but also suggests a systemic failure in standard compliance practices. An OECD co-ordinated approach is under consideration in 2015. This is a subject that will not go away.

INCREASING COMPLIANCE SPEND

Despite all these apparent regulatory and compliance failures since 2008 and the cost of rectifying them, the increase in the level of regulatory intervention and compliance recruitment and salaries has continued unabated:

> ... With starting salaries for compliance officers rising 3.5 percent each year since 2011.
> Compliance professionals in banks or broker-dealers with a couple of years of experience often make $65,000 to $85,000; five to 10 years of experience can command a base salary of up to $150,000 per year.
> JP Morgan Chase ... planned to add 3,000 employees in the compliance function, even after adding 7,000 such employees in 2013.
>> **Julie DiMauro,** *Compliance Complete* (**Thomson Reuters Accelus, December 3, 2014**)

We can see this trend across many major jurisdictions, and emerging ones, and across individual organisations from the largest to the smallest. HSBC has had to increase its compliance numbers by some 3,000 since its deferred prosecution agreement action and is being supervised by hundreds of U.S. regulatory officials. Meanwhile, at the other end of the spectrum, in Ireland the Registry of Credit Unions is insisting that even small volunteer-run credit unions take on a risk-and-compliance person, which is more than many can afford. This move is provoking credit union amalgamations and service sharing. This may be necessary, but may also undermine the very values and outcomes that credit unions were set up to deliver to local communities and that the "common-bond" concept enshrines.

A LINE IN THE SAND

These failings pre- and post-2008 have led to some new approaches across regulation within stage 3 of the General Model, attempting to draw a line in the sand so that regulation can rebuild its reputation and compliance can dig in. This is easier in jurisdictions that have not been so badly affected by the GFC.

For example, in Singapore, MAS summarised their new approaches to these challenges in the principles of effective supervision:

Principle 1: Emphasise risk-focused supervision rather than one-size-fits-all regulation.

Principle 2: Assess the adequacy of an institution's risk management in the context of its risk and business profiles.

Principle 3: Allocate scarce supervisory resources according to impact and risks.

Principle 4: Ensure institutions are supervised on an integrated (across industry) and consolidated (across geography) basis.

Principle 5: Maintain high standards in financial supervision, including observing international standards and best practices.

Principle 6: Seek to reduce the risk of failure rather than prevent the failure of any institution.

Principle 7: Place principal responsibility for risk oversight on the institution's board and management.

Principle 8: Leverage on relevant stakeholders, professionals, industry associations, and other agencies.

Principle 9: Rely on timely, accurate, and adequate disclosure by institutions rather than merit-based regulation of products to protect consumers.

Principle 10: Empower consumers to assess and assume for themselves the financial risks of their financial decisions.

Principle 11: Give due regard to competitiveness, business efficiency, and innovation.

Principle 12: Adopt a consultative approach to regulating the industry.

This consolidation within stage 3 included restating some of the tenets of traditional regulation, such as the value of:

- *New capital measures* (Basel III).
- *Extraterritorial regulation:* Sarbanes–Oxley and the Patriot Act were followed by FATCA to tackle tax avoidance, the 2010 UK Bribery Act and FATF's extra layer of AML international regulation.
- *Increased cross-border cooperation:* The GFC revealed fault-lines in the global regulation and supervision of cross-border firms; banking

institutions are global in life, but national in death. That is, when crises occur, it is national central banks that have to provide lender-of-last-resort support, and national governments that provide fiscal support.

FUTURE CHALLENGES

Future challenges facing the regulatory and compliance system are considerable, arguably greater than the challenges inherent in the 2008 GFC. These challenges relate to a growing, aging, and globalizing population, and include:

- Ring fencing (separation of retail and investment banking).
- Tax transparency.
- Shadow banking and off-exchange dealing decreases accountability.
- Economic shocks (in EU, for example) or slowdown in the BRIC countries' growth.
- Aging populations bring higher costs and pension liberalization new risks.
- Rising property prices create issues for intergenerational equity.
- Rising middle-class demands for consumer protection increase regulatory intervention and unintended consequences.
- New forms of currency may (initially) fall outside the banking system and new mobile payment methods raise new categories of risk.
- Cybercrime and data vulnerability is increasing rapidly.
- Climate change and migration.
- Oil price falls have placed strains on dependent jurisdictions.
- Low inflation/deflation and low investment returns tend towards increasing the desire for risk taking.
- Outcome-focused regulation can raise compliance issues if used retrospectively.
- Increasing diligence on sanctions.
- Regulatory arbitrage and differential reward regimes.

All of these are complex issues for compliance and make it even more important that compliance understands and adopts the new strategies set out in Part II.

CONCLUSION

The picture painted here may seem somewhat bleak. The increasing industrialization of compliance may mean more headcount but less head quality and may undermine hopes of full professionalization.

Regulators started to move into stages 4 and 5 prior to 2008 but have been overwhelmed by the recovery task. Now they are getting back on course with new priorities and expectations, in many cases having a second go at initiatives that may not have worked so well the first time around.

To get ahead, compliance requires a proper grounding in the essentials of stages 4 and 5 and to be proactive in making it happen. Compliance has in effect been let off the hook once by the intervention of events, but as regulators approach stages 4 and 5 once again, they may not be in the mood to award too many second chances.

ENDNOTES

1. D. Jackman, "The Housing Market Has No Clothes," *Financial Adviser* (June 23, 2006).
2. D. Summers, "No Return to Boom and Bust: What Brown Said When He Was Chancellor," *Guardian Online* (Sept. 11, 2008), http://www.theguardian.com /politics/2008/sep/11/gordonbrown.economy.
3. Financial Service Authority, *The Turner Review: A Regulatory Response to the Global Banking Crisis* (London: FSA, 2009) 11, http://www.fsa.gov.uk/pubs/other /turner_review.pdf.
4. Robert J. Shiller interviewed by Christopher Jeffery in *Central Banking Journal* (May 16, 2012).
5. Department for Business, Innovation & Skills, Growth Dashboard (July 18, 2014), www.gov.uk/government/uploads/system/uploads/attachment_data/file/ 337297/Growth_Dashboard_July_2014.pdf. Accessed 10-Dec-2014.
6. D. Walker et al., *A Review of Corporate Governance in UK Banks and Other Financial Industry Entities* (2009), 9, http://webarchive.nationalarchives .gov.uk/20130129110402/http://www.hm-treasury.gov.uk/d/walker_review _consultation_160709.pdf (accessed Dec. 10, 2014).
7. V. Chew, "Lehman Brothers Minibond Saga," *Government of Singapore: Singapore Infopedia* (2010), http://eresources.nlb.gov.sg/infopedia/articles/SIP _1654_2010-03-19.html.
8. http://uk.reuters.com/article/2013/12/05/uk-standard-chartered-private-bank -idUKBRE9B40HK20131205

ENDNOTES

Practice

WHAT TO DO DIFFERENTLY

Compliance needs to develop new approaches, philosophies, and techniques in practice so that it can:

- Keep pace with regulatory progress.
- Face forthcoming global challenges.

But also compliance needs to develop a momentum and agenda of its own towards more values-led, strategic, and judgment-based practice. This will allow compliance to both add and receive greater value.

In terms of the General Model, the next step is a development of regulation and compliance from stage 3 to stages 4 and 5. The changes involved are numerous and complex, but we have separated out five key elements:

Stage 4:
1. Ethics
2. Culture and conduct risk
3. Good governance

Stage 5:
4. Sustainable Outcomes
5. Community*

---

*Community may be regarded as stage 6 and falls more naturally in Part III.

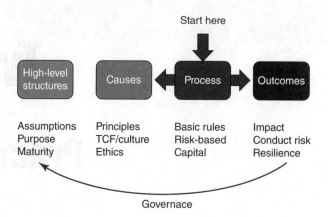

Evolution of Regulatory Focus

Having started with a focus on process, regulation moves in stage 4 to consider the causes of problems, and subsequently in stage 5 to consider the outcomes of regulatory intervention as an additional *pull factor*. The natural extension of an outcome focus is to consider the impact of firms on the wider community (a possible stage 6).

Regulation in stages 4 to 6 is delving into corporate internal workings in a more fundamentally interventionist way; together the combination of all these approaches provides a much stronger, more robust framework for maturing corporate behaviour and delivering a healthy financial and social system.

CHAPTER 4

Ethics

Without justice, society must immediately dissolve.
This avidity alone ... is ... directly destructive of society.
—David Hume, extracts from *A Treatise of Human Nature*
(1739–40)

DEFINITIONS

Ethics are the "goods" underlying all regulation and thereby compliance. The principles of justice, equity, and reasonableness are drawn from ancient traditions of ethics and philosophy. These ethics form part of the structure of society, rather than being a product of it. The principles of justice and equity underpin most common law and the secondary legislation such as regulatory rules and guidance. Regulation is thus an extension of society.

Values extend beyond ethics. Although values may include ethics, they are expressions of what is important or a priority to a firm or individual. Profitability and teamwork are values but are not necessarily ethics. Morals are the more specific positions taken by individuals or societies on ethical issues, and may change from time to time.

Principles are general statements of ethics and values together that translate ethics and values into practice. Principles are rules of thumb that are meant to be flexible to cover as many situations as possible. It is usual to talk about the *intent* behind principles, often described as the *spirit* of the principles (and the rules based on them), and this brings us back to values and then to underlying ethics.

ETHICS IN REGULATION AND COMPLIANCE

Ethics and values provide the justification for most, if not all, regulatory standards and the regulatory interventions such as supervision and enforcement used to apply them. Principles help regulators and firms understand

29

what they should do and how to do it. The partnership between the ethics and values on one side and principles on the other is about the fundamental work of compliance—translating theory into practice. Principles are necessary to set out expectations and boundary conditions and give rules of thumb that direct users towards acceptable outcomes. Ethics provide the starting point to understand direction and intent.

First it is necessary for compliance to understand and use the ethical base of their role and operations. Without an understanding of ethics, fundamentally compliance cannot be effective. It is necessary to grasp the direction the whole body of regulatory rules and standards are moving towards and the basic intent behind the spirit of the rules. Increasingly regulator and enforcement decisions draw upon understandings of intent—the intent of the firm and the intent of the rules and principles.

Compliance, as the name suggests, revolves around ensuring firms are in accord with externally set parameters and standards. These standards do not have a separate existence but represent and consolidate the expectations of the society in which the industry operates. These expectations are transmitted through elected government and its appointed regulators. They also reflect and encapsulate international norms of behaviour. All of these, given human nature, will draw upon for their justification and ultimate rationale some concept of ethics—or commonly held views of what is right and good.

It is best to see these as universal in application, although there may be some variation from culture to culture and time to time. In essence our human, common sense of ethics is that they are constant and generally understood, although not always articulated or represented in the same way. It is becoming clearer that the argument of cultural exceptions cannot be reasonably used as an excuse to override, ignore, or subvert generally recognised universal ethics. This process of recognition and clarification can be through general and wide discourse or codified in international agreements and standards and within the pronouncements of international regulatory and professional bodies.

AN ETHICAL FRAMEWORK FOR FINANCIAL SERVICES

If compliance rests on ethics, what are these ethics?

The author set out to define the core ethics of regulation for the first time for the then-newly formed single regulatory body in the UK, the Financial Services Authority (FSA). These were defined following a detailed trawl of the existing legislation, the Financial Services and Markets Act (2000), the FSA's Principles for Businesses and Principles for Individuals, and other relevant and international standards. It became evident in this process that a coherent body of ethical principles underpinned the regulatory approach, and we can safely assume these principles were in the minds of the original draughtsmen and -women.

The following Ethical Framework for Financial Services is set out in FSA Discussion Paper 18 (2002):

- Open, honest, responsive, and accountable
- Committed to acting competently, responsibly, and reliably
- Relating to colleagues and customers fairly and with respect[1]

These core ethics cover how a firm is to behave, how it should treat its customers, and how it should operate in the marketplace. In truth, not all these principles are *pure ethics*, in that openness, for example, is a practical outworking of an intention to be honest and responsible. This is not meant to be a checklist. The important point is that the phrases interrelate and provide an interwoven basis for all subsequent regulation and compliance standards. Fairness or concepts of equity remain central to this formulation. The term "Treating Customers Fairly" became the centrepiece of a major retail initiative for FSA from 2006 and continues to do so under FCA. This was followed by a similar set of regulations in Singapore: Guidance to the Financial Advisers Act. This has recently been extended as part of the Fair review.

ETHICS IN BUSINESS

Ethics helps compliance to apply regulatory principles and rules as they explain the underlying ideas behind the intent and effect of these principles, and the rules or guidance that are based on them. Ethics is an important, but not the sole, *root cause*.

Ethics is widely understood, if instinctively rather than consciously, and so provides a simple way to explain compliance requirements to staff, shareholders, and consumers alike. But crucially, ethics allows a firm to combine regulatory ethics with its own wider set of values (which may go well beyond regulatory requirements) to produce a business-friendly set of values. This combined set of ethics and ethical values provides the starting point for the convergence of regulatory and business objectives that is so crucial to successful compliance and the establishment of a compliance- and values-led corporate culture, as we will see in the next chapter.

Ethics is the starting point for "new compliance" and defines all subsequent approaches in this book. Compliance must understand ethics as a starting point for all that follows in stages 4 and 5.

HOW SHOULD A COMPLIANCE PRACTITIONER APPROACH ETHICS?

The first step is to understand what ethics are and establish a list of examples of ethics that apply in a firm.

These might start with core ethics such as:

- Fairness or equity
- Honesty
- Responsibility
- Reliability
- Care

These should then lead to *derivative ethics* or *secondary ethics*—ethics that expand upon the core ethics, but, importantly, depend upon the core ethics for their ultimate justification.

For example, *openness* and *transparency* are often stated as ethics but they are essentially ways of ensuring or demonstrating honesty. They do not have such a strong philosophical justification as core ethics but add strength and weight to *honesty*.

Many other ethics can be unpacked to give greater explanation and thereby usefulness. For example, reliability may well include the concepts of competence, promptness, prudent management, and delivery of promised results.

Some ethics terms, such as *responsibility*, are so broad that they need immediate qualification, such as responsibility to whom—usually shareholders, stakeholders, and so on.

Try to define your firm's ethics. An organisation's ethics may be different from your own or those of your colleagues. There are many reasons for this, often based on whom you are responsible for, which will be different from whom the firm is responsible to and for.

Define your own ethics:

Are they different from

- Colleagues in compliance/other parts of the business?
- The firm's collective ethics?

If so, why?

- What difference does this make to you, your firm, and how you work?
- How do these differences appear in practice?
- Who notices?
- Do you do anything about these differences?
- What are the long-term implications?

ETHICS AT WORK VERSUS ETHICS AT HOME

How are your ethics different at home or amongst friends compared to ethics at work? It can be the case that individuals' ethics change when they come to work, possibly in a case of playing up to expectations. Staff can leave their good intentions at the front door. Part of ethics initiatives in firms is to reinstate the sorts of ethics you would have exercised at home. For example, an approach to alter ethics in a firm may start with questions like:

- Would you treat your family in this way?
- Would you sell this product to your mother? (the "mom test")
- Would you be happy for your friends to see what you do at work?
- Would you be happy for the media to report what you said/did?

The final point widens the test and is asking how you think your actions match up to what you understand to be the general standards and ethics of the community or society. This can be very helpful on its own but it is important to question the motivation here. Is the shift to a more ethical standpoint and forms of behaviour a result of fear of being caught-out or suffering reputational damage, or do you act ethically because you want to?

The thesis here is that only the second is truly ethical, and only internally driven ethics, not externally imposed ethics, will be long lasting, effective, and hold up under pressure. This focus on individual and corporate intent will form the focus of the next chapter and is of crucial importance to the regulator and how it judges a firm or carries out enforcement. It is also clear to how staff and customers view the firm. Different drivers of intent determine how a firm may then seek to develop its ethics and embed ethical culture. Different techniques will be used if the motivation is fear based; more nurturing and empowering methodologies are possible if the primary driver is from within. Similarly, a regulator can work with a firm differently depending on whether it is reactive or values-led.

STEPS TOWARDS DEVELOPING ETHICS

"Finding good" is a long and difficult path. You may find inspiration for what ethics matter in your business during a conversation with a client, or over a meal with colleagues, or from hammering out a difficult decision in a meeting. You may be disillusioned by what you discover is actually going on in a certain part of the business and this may spur you on to be clearer about what ethics are acceptable.

You may think through what matters to your business in a team away-day, as being apart from the daily turmoil is always refreshing, or you may be able to think more clearly on your own on a quiet walk, or travelling home, or talking through issues away from work. Those who think about "good" at any length often find that they develop an eye or a greater sensitivity for ethical issues and a sensibility that others may not share. The problem is making ethics real and effective, not an academic debate or occasional interest. In order to achieve this richness of thought and consideration and to spread this as widely as possible the following key steps are suggested:

1. Develop a common understanding about what constitutes being ethical within compliance.
2. Ensure this aligns with regulatory expectations and business expectations.
3. Test your understanding with related departments such as legal and HR and in the line.
4. Gain board support, especially from friendly non-executive directors.
5. Pilot an ethical approach in a small area or division.
6. Roll out to all staff.
7. Publicise or demonstrate to the regulator and other stakeholders, especially customers.
8. Continue to evolve, test, and update.

Note that "the tone at the top" and "walking the talk" are vital and a lack of support or poor examples of behaviour from compliance and other managers can undermine any initiative in ethics rapidly. For any individual trying to be ethical it is undermining to see colleagues opt out or find shortcuts.

The key point is that being ethical is not an incidental add-on. It needs to sit right at the core of all you and your colleagues do. It is a collective more than an individual effort. How you bounce ideas off each other matters as much as the stand that any one individual might take. Working on ethics alone can be lonely and not very effective.

The difference is probably transparent to a customer between being confronted by a member of staff driven to make any sale at any cost regardless of suitability, and a professional advisor with a genuine desire to provide quality, objective, professional advice and a helpful service. The latter is worth a lot in current market conditions and builds trust in the practitioner, the firm, and the industry. This is also what the regulator wants to achieve.

MAIN TOOLS FOR IDENTIFYING AND APPLYING CORPORATE ETHICS

In this chapter we consider the first three of the tools listed here. The remainder are more closely related to the embedding of ethical culture and outcomes, considered in Chapters 5 and 7:

1. **Writing an ethics code**
2. **Ethics training**
3. **Ethical decision making**
4. Ethics communication—reinforcing good-news stories
5. Ethics leadership—tone at the top
6. Ethics database of useful precedents and learning points
7. Systems, policies, and controls supporting ethics
8. Ethics reward in bonuses and career promotion

These tools or interventions need to be interlinked and reinforcing each other to create a supportive and effective ethical environment. Cynicism is easy and any dissonance or unconformity will undermine the entire effort and put back the journey. This chapter will focus on the first three tools listed here, but all of them will be developed over the course of subsequent chapters as they pull in additional factors that have become important in later stages of regulatory and compliance development, such as culture, governance, and outcomes.

THREE CRITICAL STEPS IN ESTABLISHING ETHICS

Here are the three most important first steps:

Step 1: Writing an ethics code

Step 2: Ethics training

Step 3: Ethical decision making

In what follows, we help you to work through each of them.

Step 1: Writing an Ethics Code

The first step is to set out your corporate ethics in some sort of code. There are many types, from short lists to prescriptive lists of acceptable behaviours.

However, ethics codes are not the same as *codes of conduct*. These may set out a firm's policies on personal account dealing and grievances. These are *internal-facing* procedures that may be ethics based but are not to be confused with an ethics code.

We provide three examples here to show something of the range: one large company, one small, and one a generic bank code you could use and adapt.

EXAMPLE 1: A LARGE COMPANY—LLOYD'S INSURANCE MARKET

Ethical behaviour underpins the way we behave, do business, and treat one another. Our values determine our behaviour and we must support and uphold them so that they are an integral part of day-to-day life. This code aims to guide our actions and those of people with whom we work closely, encouraging a way of working that is honest, responsible, and respectful, generating trust. We ensure that the standards in this code are communicated to and understood by the participants.

Conduct:

- We are open and honest and try to act fairly.
- We comply with legal, regulatory, and license requirements.
- We do not tolerate corruption in any form, whether direct or indirect.
- We compete vigorously but honestly, observing proper standards of market conduct.
- We respect the confidentiality of information disclosed to us in confidence.
- High standards of corporate governance are integral to the way we manage our business.

People:

- We treat people with fairness, respect, and decency.
- We help employees to develop their potential.
- We do not discriminate on any grounds other than the ability to work effectively.
- We provide healthy, safe, and secure work environments.

Environment and Community:

- We contribute to the social and economic wellbeing of those communities where we are an employer.
- We listen to neighbouring communities and take account of their interests.
- We work to minimise the adverse environmental impact of our business operations.

EXAMPLE 2: A SMALL FIRM—WALTERS & SHEK IFA

We will:

1. Help you to the best of our ability.
2. Not take advantage of your inexperience.
3. Communicate as clearly as we can and try and be in good time.
4. Give you all the information you need to reach a sound decision.
5. Correct as swiftly as possible any mistakes of our own.
6. Be considerate when others make mistakes.
7. Give you what you pay for.

EXAMPLE 3: A GENERIC CODE FOR A BANK

1. Relationships of trust are at the heart of all we do.
2. We treat all our clients with care and respect.
3. We safeguard our clients' best interests and are good stewards of their assets.
4. We aim to deliver the highest levels of expertise and service.
5. We tell it straight: no spin, no obscuring.
6. We make decisions on the basis of merit and principle and stand accountable.

7. Our ethics and professionalism mean that sometimes we have to say "no."
8. We inspire a wealth of possibilities, seeing what really matters, not merely ticking a box.
9. We are rooted in community, fostering sustainability and prosperity.
10. We choose to do the right thing because we want to, not merely because we should.

Now try to devise your own ethics code:

1. _____.

2. _____.

3. _____.

Sources of Reference for an Ethical Code You may find it useful to consider some of the following.

General Ethical Principles

- *Client needs:* Placing the client's best interests at the heart of the business and maintaining a position of trust founded on proven professionalism is often a starting point. But as this can be aspirational and unrealistic, we need to *balance* the interests of the firm and the customer.
- *Honesty and integrity:* We conduct our business at all times with the utmost honesty and integrity. We will not place ourselves in any situation where our professionalism could be questioned or where our actions, decisions, or omissions may damage the reputation of the firm or the financial services industry as a whole. This may mean declining business.
- *Fairness:* Find the right balance between our need to remain profitable and the client's needs by setting and communicating reasonable expectations, rights, responsibilities, and values. Recognising this requires quality judgment on a daily basis and may require input from many stakeholders, and full resources to be utilised to resolve often complex issues and choices, from designing products and services to operating after-sales support. In all of these, the staff that delivers equitable, just, sustainable good outcomes shall be rewarded.

- *Objectivity:* Make judgments objectively and independently, based on all the relevant information available and on merit; be aware of the wider context and seeking to balance long- and short-term considerations while demonstrably setting aside any self-interest and declaring appropriately any possible conflicts of interest. This may mean a deeper examination of issues, rather than reaching for a quick-fix or ticking the box and then moving on without a thorough follow-through and ongoing responsibility.
- *Openness and accountability:* Ensure that others understand what we do. The information we provide must be clear and straightforward and the reasons for our individual and the firm's decisions and actions should be accessible and unobstructed in any way beyond established necessary confidentiality. Our basis of remuneration, reward, and appraisal should be fair, open, and objective. We listen to and understand the needs, expectations, and concerns (and complaints) of our stakeholders and have many ways of ensuring easy, accessible, and continuing engagement.
- *Responsibility and ownership:* Make everyone's responsibilities clear and define what they should do if they reach the boundaries of their responsibilities or level of expertise. We encourage everyone in the firm to address, make, and own difficult decisions (within the bounds of their defined responsibilities) regularly and consistently, bringing to bear the firm's values and ethics as an established part of everyday behaviour. Everyone in the firm is prepared to challenge, explain, and be accountable for any decision or action or lack of either.
- *Respect for others:* Understand the values and position of others, not discriminating against any person regardless of race or racial group; sex or sexual orientation; religion or belief; age; and disability; or bringing any undue pressure to bear.
- *Stewardship:* Safeguard all resources prudently and proactively, remaining alert and sanguine to avoid undue risk, observing the spirit and the principles of all applicable laws, regulations, good market conduct, and established best practice, both national and international. Incorporate at all levels an outward-looking, responsive learning culture that is sensitive to the role played by the firm in the wider economy and society, and bring into focus and measure the impact that financial services outcomes can have on strengthening individuals and communities.
- *Leadership and teamwork:* Lead the industry as a values-based, ethical, and professional financial institution providing the highest quality independent advice, and make a substantial contribution to rebuilding trust and confidence in the financial services industry. We apply these same values within the firm—walking the talk at all levels.

Ten General Principles of Public Life These UK standards are widely referred to:

1. *Selflessness:* Members should serve only the public interest and should never improperly confer an advantage or disadvantage on any person.
2. *Honesty and integrity:* Members should not place themselves in situations where their honesty and integrity may be questioned, should not behave improperly, and should on all occasions avoid the appearance of such behavior.
3. *Objectivity:* Members should make decisions on merit, including when making appointments, awarding contracts, or recommending individuals for rewards or benefits.
4. *Accountability:* Members should be accountable to the public for their actions and the manner in which they carry out their responsibilities, and should cooperate fully and honestly with any scrutiny appropriate to their particular office.
5. *Openness:* Members should be as open as possible about their actions and those of their authority, and should be prepared to give reasons for those actions.
6. *Personal judgment:* Members may take account of the views of others, including their political groups, but should reach their own conclusions on the issues before them and act in accordance with those conclusions.
7. *Respect for others:* Members should promote equality by not discriminating unlawfully against any person, and by treating people with respect, regardless of their race, age, religion, gender, sexual orientation, or disability. They should respect the impartiality and integrity of the authority's statutory officers and its other employees.
8. *Duty to uphold the law:* Members should uphold the law and, on all occasions, act in accordance with the trust that the public is entitled to place in them.
9. *Stewardship:* Members should do what they can to ensure that their authorities use their resources prudently and in accordance with the law.
10. *Leadership:* Members should promote and support these principles by leadership and by example, and should act in a way that secures or preserves public confidence.

Industry and Professional Standards There are many sector standards developed for organisations or used on a voluntary basis. For example, the International Compliance Association (ICA), the professional body for compliance worldwide, is in the process of introducing a new ethics code, prepared by the author, which has relevance to all compliance officers in any jurisdiction or sector.

The International Compliance Association (ICA) Code 2015:

1. Compliance holds a unique and significant position between the firm and the relevant regulatory authorities. Compliance professionals need to be clear and transparent about their responsibilities to both and the limitations of their scope.
2. The integrity and effectiveness of compliance is founded on an independence of thought and judgment. Compliance professionals should protect and enhance their independence and alert senior management or regulators should this independence be compromised.
3. Compliance professionals should be proactive in building a positive ethos and culture in their firm that understands, respects, and is committed to regulatory objectives, values, and outcomes.
4. Within a mature compliance culture, it should be possible and encouraged to raise uncomfortable issues and ask challenging questions. Compliance professionals should contribute to enabling constructive challenge at all levels in the organization and value the contributions made.
5. Compliance professionals should find opportunities to uncover and consider the spirit and intent of regulations, and avoid tick-boxes and other methods of oversimplification that diminish the value and importance of compliance.
6. Professionalism requires mature judgment in balancing competing priorities and differing responsibilities, interpreting grey areas, and making final decisions. Compliance professionals should not shy away from such difficult decisions and recognize that sound judgments form the basis of compliance's strategic value and impact.
7. Transparency is unconditional. Compliance should have access to any information and remain committed to open, clear, accurate, timely, and accessible reporting internally and to regulators.
8. Compliance professionals should strive to have open relationships with colleagues, offering high-quality advice and guidance, yet understand where ownership of risk lies and not overly protect colleagues from difficult decisions that must be owned.
9. Compliance professionals should have direct access to or representation on the main board or its equivalent with a role that includes regular briefings, induction, training, horizon scanning, compliance planning, and regulatory risk management.
10. Compliance professionals have a responsibility to develop their own competence through appropriate qualifications and updating, to never exceed the limitations of their competence, and to assist in the education and development of other members.

These sources and many others should help you draw up your own code.

How to Use Your Ethics Code While an ethics code will not solve every problem and may have little effect on its own, it is a useful starting point for compliance and for business more generally. It is hard, given public expectations of corporate organisations, to justify not having an ethics code.

This code gives compliance a starting point, a point of reference. It should not be a new set of rules and should not be applied or discussed and analysed in the same way. A problem comes from being too detailed and prescriptive but a different problem comes from being too smart and possibly trite. An overly contrived code can seem remote and be difficult for staff to remember.

You will need to think about ways of helping staff to be recalling the code on a regular basis or when it is relevant, such as having it as a screen-saver, or putting posters on walls or by vending machines. More useful is having a version that can be attached to board papers or meeting papers so it can be referred to easily.

Once an ethics code is public, any customer or stakeholder can hold you or the firm to it. This raises the stakes, so it is important that:

- Everyone in the firm knows the code or where to find it.
- The code is achievable.
- The code is monitored.
- Everyone is committed to the code.
- The code is supported from the top.
- The code is used in induction and training.
- The firm reports on how well the code operates, openly and regularly.

To obviously and publicly fail to achieve the aspirations of an ethics code is very undermining and can lead to cynicism, to the extent that some might argue it is less desirable to have an ethics code at all. But nowadays it seems remiss for any sizeable organisation not to have an ethics code and it is on balance more damaging as the lack of a code suggests disinterest in customers and ethics.

It is important for all to remember that codes are aspirational, mistakes will happen, and they are not meant to be the same as rules. If they start becoming a source of bureaucracy and box-ticking, then you are going in the wrong direction.

Step 2: Ethics Training

Education is key to successful ethics and successful compliance. There is much misunderstanding on the subject of ethics education. It is not possible to train in ethics. You can build awareness of ethical issues, practice dealing with difficult situations, and share experiences and ethical solutions or ideas, but this is no substitute for involving ethics in daily work, and this is why we put more emphasis on tool 3.

We are also sceptical about assessing someone's ethics on recruitment or at any stage. Such evaluations may be useful, but just like other psychological testing, it is open to candidates' seeking to give a favourable impression. Overall corporate ethics is a collective characteristic and what matters to consumer and regulator is how people act together and affect each other. This is the basis of the development of this area into a focus on culture, explained in the next chapter.

Types of Training

1. Induction—when staff join the firm
2. Board or senior management briefings:
   - Provide an overview of the increased regulatory emphasis on ethical behavior.
   - Outline the opportunities in establishing a distinctive ethical/values edge.
   - Explain how challenge frameworks operate.
   - Confirm common core values and vision.
3. Examination courses—in qualifications
4. Staff training programme:
   - The value of ethics in business
   - How to use ethics frameworks and challenge processes
   - How to sustain ethos and culture, especially in difficult situations
   - Evaluation, management information, and customer satisfaction
5. Regular ethics updating on new issues:
   - Frontline advice giving
   - Management systems and controls, collection of MI, risk management
   - HR and training, reward, and appraisal

Example Training Programme A typical staff-training programme might cover:

1. *Introduction to ethics:* 30 min, scene setting
   - What are ethics and values? (discussion)
   - Why is ethics important to business and to regulation?
   - The regulatory drivers examples of poor culture, reputational risk
   - International examples

2. *The ethics journey:* 30 min
   - Key steps
   - What does success look like? (critical success factors)
   - What will/can we measure?
   - Indicators and changing relationships

3. *Implementing ethics:* 1 hour, 15 min, in-depth explanation of use of tools
   - What does the *ethics code* mean?
   - How *ethics questions* can be used in everyday situations
   - How to keep ethics fresh (discussion)
   - How to resolve difficult issues

4. *Individual ownership:* 45 min, small groups
   - What it means to be a professional: professional standards and codes
   - Being put on the spot
   - Involving and supporting others: Where can we find help? (ethics committee)
   - Ethics case log, evaluation, and reward
   - How can values add value?

5. *Case studies:* Two sessions of 30 min each on relevant case examples

6. *Conclusion:* Creating space for ethics to work—plenary: 30 min
   - Raising issues that could either help or be blockers
   - A more principles-based approach to advice
   - Connections (e.g., Bribery Act)
   - Discussion and questions
   - Next steps—using the ethics systems

ETHICAL EXERCISES—SOME EXAMPLES

Here are some scenarios or case studies you could use (based on real cases):

Exercise 1

A family have recently inherited £750k and are looking for financial advice. They do not own a house but are long-term tenants with rent of £1,900pcm. They have a good credit history and £35k savings, a £25k loan and £15k outstanding on credit cards. Their small business banks with another bank and earns revenues of around £110k, with minimal costs of £5k. They have one child left at private school with two years to run at £10k per term, one child at university in the United States, and one starting work. They have 10 years of minimal pension contributions in a pension plan and 10 years in a final salary scheme. They are open to higher levels of risk.

- How can the bank help them?
- What would be an "ethical outcome"?

Exercise 2

A promising young person, just graduated, 22, is a prospective client. He has available in trusts at least £60k and has some interesting business start-up ideas he wants to discuss. His friends and potential business partners may have access to considerable additional capital. All concerned have the usual level of student debt liability and share a house owned by one. They are conscious of their own values and are concerned to work with a bank that takes ethics in business seriously.

- How would you deal with them?
- How, specifically, would you respond to their ethical concerns?

Exercise 3

A new business venture, to be funded privately, is looking for additional capital. The loan required is £150k, half the amount required to purchase a hotel premises on a 25-year lease basis. The business plan is coherent and credible on an ongoing basis and there is potential to convert adjacent buildings and expand. The loan can be almost entirely secured on private property but there is a shortfall in available working capital. The existing business earns £80–100k gross profit on 50 percent occupancy.

- What are your initial thoughts about such a proposition? Where do ethics come in?
- What further considerations would arise in making a decision?

Use these as starting points to develop your own case studies.

Step 3: Ethical Decision Making

This is the crucial step—critical to the quality of decision making throughout an organisation and to the quality of compliance.

There is rarely such a instance as a purely ethical question or a solely ethical dilemma. Even though there are many ethical resolution tools and ethical decision-making exercises and training courses or even ethics exams, these are all far too abstracted from the pressures of everyday situations.

It is always necessary to find a way of weighing up and bringing together influences and information from many sources. These may be ethically informed and as we have seen the regulatory foundations are almost always ethically based. But the process is much more complex than that. You need to bring into play as many sources of reference as possible:

- Rulebooks
- Precedents
- Standards from other sectors or international bodies
- Regulatory speeches and statements
- Recorded conversations with regulators
- Correspondence with regulators

These give bearings towards finding an acceptable ethical position in a method that resembles triangulation used in mapmaking and route finding (i.e., working from at least two known points to provide a basis for deciding where you should be located; see Figure 4.1).This process of triangulation provides an area in which it is safe and ethical for the firm to operate and it can choose a number of different positions if it wishes to differentiate its ethical position slightly. In terms of compliance the more reference points the better.

Decision making and the recording of the decisions now become key for compliance. The challenge is: How do you bring such complex decision making to the fore in everyday situations?

The main technique used is a structure of questions that touch ethical issues or encourage users to connect with broader principles, gates or windows through to the underlying issues. These sets of questions are structured,

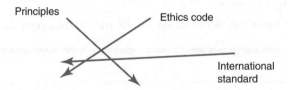

FIGURE 4.1 Triangulation to Find Ethical Position

following major ethical themes, and interlock in exactly the same way as triangulation so they give a number of fixes on a possible position. Using these regularly aids consistency and improves the quality of ethical decision making. Users become more mature in their use of the questions, selecting the best-fit set and adding their own.

The following comprises a library from which you can select your 10 most useful questions (10 is about as many as you should have in a working list). They could be used at board meetings as well as compliance meetings and client meetings.

Framework Challenge Process Here is an example of a structured challenge process you can try out.

1. Trust and care:
   - Do others trust us? Should they?
   - How will this action foster trust and build relationships?
   - Under pressure, do we swap cooperation for coercion—in the team and beyond?
   - Do they feel I/we care?

2. Openness:
   - Are we keeping anyone in the dark? If so, why? Who else should we involve?
   - How do we help others to understand us?
   - Why would we ever want to use legalese or small print?
   - Are we dodging the decision or hiding behind process?
   - Do we worry what might be found out?
   - Do we report all we should? How about conflicts of interest and remuneration?
   - Would we be happy to have anyone from outside here, including the press?
   - Is openness real only when someone asks ... ?

3. Fairness:
   - Who benefits, and should they? Who loses out?
   - Do we value our existing customers as much as potential new ones?
   - Is this how we would like to be treated?
   - Whose money is it?
   - Are we responsible and prudent only when it costs us nothing?
   - Do we deliver what we say we will do? Do we stand by our commitments?
   - Are we up to the job, or should we refer on?
   - Are we as qualified as we need to be?

4. Values-led:
   - What is our key driver? Is it worthwhile, and it is ethical?
   - Can we remove prescription to an extent to allow people to make (and own) their ethical decisions?
   - If we look hard, is there an implied or inbuilt prejudice here? Could this be oppressive to someone?
   - Do we look for ethical principles to fill the gaps, or must we find a box to tick?
   - Where do our principles come from? Do they need to flex, or are they being used too flexibly?

5. Integrity:
   - Do our ethics mean that we should count this out right at the beginning?
   - Is our challenge process robust and secure enough? Does anyone feel reticent to speak out?
   - Have we learned from our mistakes, looking across the group? How do we help others understand us?
   - Is something being pushed through without proper discussion /analysis? If so, why?
   - Is there any evidence that contrary, possibly "non-corporate" views have been ignored, marginalised, compromised?
   - Does the bottom-line driver obscure other even more important issues?

6. Responsibility:
   - What are the wider outcomes for all stakeholders?
   - What are our responsibilities? Are they being upheld?
   - What are the responsibilities of other parties? Do they see these?
   - What are the wider, collective benefits?
   - Do we have rights? What do rights really mean?
   - Can we scope out the grey areas and identify a range of good outcomes?

7. Insight:
   - Are we being incisive?
   - Are we just ticking boxes?
   - What really matters in the situation we are in?
   - Can we see through the black box to the underlying principles? Can our customers?
   - What is the elephant in the room?
   - Do we act as machines processing numbers, or people relating to people?

- Do we hide behind form-filling and process?
- What is the bigger picture?

8. Sustainability:

   - What are the outcomes in the short and the long term? How can we weigh these?
   - How can we build in resilience for the long term?
   - Are our principles laid aside when we are under pressure or when we see an apparently good opportunity?
   - How should we change to more clearly reflect our values?
   - Does the status quo represent a fear of change, self-interest, or the paralysis of fear of failure?
   - What is undue return or a "quick buck"?

9. Communities:

   - Who or where is our community?
   - Are values in our community changing?
   - What does community need and what is its potential?
   - Do we engage with our stakeholders on sufferance, when we have to, or continually and with a purpose? Do we listen and learn?
   - What is our role and overall purpose?
   - What does sustainable development mean?
   - What does it mean to belong?

10. Being ethical:

   - Do we have widely held values-led vision and an understanding of ethical outcomes?
   - Are we consistent in our values across the group?
   - Could there be a mismatch between our external values and our internal behaviour? Do we walk the talk?
   - Are our values obvious and transparent to anyone who does not know us?
   - Are there any other reference points that give us a baseline or starting point?
   - Do we apply ethical criteria simply to gain an advantage or because we believe it is the right thing to do?

Now consider:

1. What questions worked for you?
2. What questions would you add?
3. What situations could you use these questions in?
4. How would you encourage their use?

The concept is that these questions, or a subset of them, become standing agenda items for team meetings, one-to-one meetings, adviser–client meetings, and even board meetings (see connection with constructive challenge in governance). These questions prompt intelligent and insightful discussion about the ethical content of issues and allow sometimes-difficult subjects to be raised in an unthreatening way. It also removes the embarrassment or fear of career limitation an individual may experience in raising their head above the parapet and asking questions that perhaps everyone or nobody wants to ask.

The previous list can be condensed, adapted, and refined for your own company. It should be regularly updated and revalidated to ensure it is empowering debate. Here is one company example currently in use, and then you can try to devise your own list.

COMPANY EXAMPLE—ROYAL BANK OF SCOTLAND'S "YES CHECK" IN THE COMPANY'S CODE OF CONDUCT

Our customers, colleagues, and the communities in which we do business trust each of us to be thoughtful and professional in everything we do. They expect each of us to exercise good judgment and do the right thing. We use our values to help think through decisions and make sure we do the right thing. When in doubt, we use the Yes Check for guidance.

Decisions are not always straightforward. The Yes Check can help us. It's a tool, not a rule.

Ask yourself:

1. Does what I am doing keep our customers and the bank safe and secure? Consider the impact of what you are doing. Rehearse a briefing with your boss.

2. Would customers and colleagues say I am acting with integrity? Consider: Would I do this to someone in my family or a friend?

3. Would I do it to myself? Am I happy with how this would be perceived on the outside? Consider the impact of this in the outside world. Try writing the press release. Does it sound good for customers?

4. Is what I am doing meeting the standards of conduct required? Think: if you are unsure, seek a second opinion.

5. In five years' time, would others see this as a good way to work? Will this have a positive impact?[2]

Specific Dilemma Resolution It is possible to think of this questioning process as a continuous cycle that allows you to bring in ethics and principles from many sources. It is usual, however, that ethical issues are not isolated but are part of a complex interrelationship of interconnected problems and considerations that makes such a stylised tool more theoretical than practical, but it can assist. (See Figure 4.2.)

This is an iterative process: you may repeat this cycle several times and refine your answer. Also you may find it useful to work inward from extremes, deciding the worst case and the best case in each stage and then deciding what central position can be achieved in practice. This is not the same as a compromise, as you try to stay true to the principles. The ethical principles at stake can be many and varied. It is simply not possible (or appropriate) to give an exhaustive list here, so it is up to firms and individuals to work on building up a case file on issues that have arisen in their firm and in the sector (or occasionally outside the sector).

Further Ethics Exercises Here are a variety of hypothetical situations to illustrate where it might not be easy to decide what the right course of action might be. They are very short as they are essentially thought-starters to be used as part of a wider discussion about ethical behaviour more generally, which you may wish to have with your colleagues.

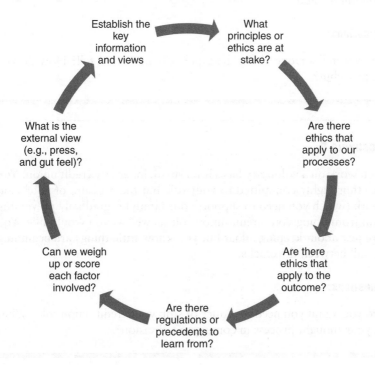

FIGURE 4.2 Ethical Questioning as a Continuous Cycle

Scenario 1

You live and work in London where a major disaster has affected settlement of credit card withdrawals to such an extent that they may never be settled. This has not stopped people flocking to ATMs to withdraw cash, hoping that they will be getting money for nothing.

Questions:

Would you join in? Would you tell others?

Scenario 2

You work in the compliance area of a large securities firm. A tape is sent to you anonymously that appears to be the recording of a conversation between two of your firm's staff. In it, the staff members seem to be discussing the weak controls in one area of the firm and colluding to commit a fraud.

Questions:

Do you tell anyone about the tape? Whom do you tell? How do you approach it?

Scenario 3

You work on a voluntary basis for a small, inner-city credit union. You are thoroughly committed to your role but the pressure of your paid work (which you need to support your family) is gradually preventing you from doing your credit union role as well as you would like. You are just about keeping afloat but you know little things are beginning to fall between the cracks.

Questions:

Do you admit you need to reduce or stop your credit union role? What is your thought process in coming to a decision?

Scenario 4

You work in a senior role in financial control in a life assurance firm. The CEO has asked you to propose a downsizing of the firm as costs are spiralling. He has asked you to be informed in your decision by employees' performance appraisals of the last two years.

You notice that in some areas some employees have not been formally assessed for performance over that period. You raise this with the CEO, who tells you to just decide on the basis of salary as everyone in that division is not meeting their targets.

Questions:

What's the right thing to do? Can you do the right thing without making your position at the firm untenable?

Scenario 5

You are a journalist for the city department of an evening newspaper. Pickings are a bit light one day and your city editor tells you he heard rumours of a big city takeover involving two large investment banks. You explain that you have good, reliable contacts with these firms and had heard nothing. Your editor concedes that there really is no rumour, yet insists nonetheless that you run a speculative headline and tells you to "make it sound real."

Questions;

What do you say to your boss? If he doesn't listen, what do you do next?

Scenario 6

You have been taken on as a financial consultant in a medium-sized firm, Independent Financial Advisors. You are asked in your first week of employment to navigate around the firm's IT systems to familiarize yourself with them. To your surprise, you come across some memo exchanges that appear to admit that the firm widely mis-sold a certain type of bond during the past 12 months but was now going back over client "fact-finds" so that the mis-selling might not look so obvious. You are aware that the FSA is shortly due to visit to look at the selling practices of your firm.

Questions:

Do you alert anyone to your discovery? If so, whom?

Scenario 7

You are employed as a customer service assistant in a call centre credit card operation for a major UK bank. You receive a complaint over the phone from a customer who claims that he has wrongly been debited £10 for an annual credit card fee when the card he was issued carried no fee. You confirm with the customer that this will be dealt with and move to amend the onscreen details. However, you remember your supervisor having told you a week or so before that given the firm's tight financial position, you should only action a customer complaint if he/she complains more than once about the same matter—even though you know this is contrary to written call centre procedures. You know that more of your calls and entries are being routinely monitored.

Questions:

Do you action the customer's complaint? What are the issues you need to consider? What could be the impact for you?

Scenario 8

A friend tells you how he has just obtained £4,000 interest-free credit by getting a new credit card. He was supposed to have transferred an outstanding balance from another card to get it but the company did not check and just gave him the amount he had asked for. He did not intend to keep the card beyond the six months credit-free period. He suggested you should do the same.

Questions:

Do you consider taking advantage of the offer? Are there any ethical considerations here?

Scenario 9

You are a project manager for an Internet portal. You are selecting a project team for a major piece of work that could last up to six months. Your boss has recommended you make use of a particular member of staff who has much of the technical skills you need. However, from past experience, you know that this person has difficulty working in a team, tends to turn up at important meetings late or get the date wrong, and you had difficulty communicating this to him last time you managed him on a project.

Questions:

Do you raise the issue with your boss? What are your considerations?

Scenario 10

You work in a corporate finance firm and you have accompanied your immediate boss to a late-afternoon meeting with clients at a top-notch hotel. There is more to discuss than you first realised, so the meeting spills over into dinner.

Your clients are staying overnight in the hotel. Your boss goes to the bar with the most senior client and comes back on his own. He asks you to go to the client's room to discuss the proposed deal further and to "give him the personal touch."

Questions:

How do you respond in this situation? What could you say to your boss, assuming you wanted to defuse the situation?

Scenario 11

You run a successful but small treasury operation for a bank with a good reputation for ethical practice. A close family friend is worried about his son's job prospects and exhorts you to take him on even though there are many more suitably qualified candidates for the advertised role.

Question:

What would you say to your friend?

Scenario 12

In your spare time, you do a lot of administration for a charitable organisation in your home area. The organisation clearly wants to keep overhead as low as possible so as to give as much money to its cause as it can. You often find yourself in the office of the mortgage advisor you work for after hours, wading through the admin. You often forget to bring the necessary equipment with you, so find yourself using the office stationery and equipment, such as staplers, CDs, wallet files, and so on. You're not sure how you feel about this but try to avoid being seen doing it.

Question:

Is this okay as long as it's only a small amount of stationery or is there a more fundamental issue here?

ETHICS IN REGULATION

There are few direct references to ethics in regulation despite the fact that the entire structure is built on ethics. Ethics, in the generalised form of integrity, appears in most rulebooks as part of a fit and proper test for individuals and threshold conditions for admitting firms. These provisions are often high level and just allow for negatives to be identified to block admission or registration (e.g., if an individual has a criminal record or outstanding debt).

They do not act as much of a sieve or a compulsion to greater ethical activity.

The FCA rulebook, as part of its training and competence requirements, has included ethics as a basic requirement:

> ... competence means having the skills, knowledge and expertise needed to discharge the responsibilities of an employee's role. This includes achieving a good standard of ethical behaviour.[3]

This applies to individuals and is backed up in independent consumer advice sectors by the requirement to have an SPS—a Statement of Professional Standing—in which practitioners have to declare that they are ethical and hold relevant qualifications. Consideration is currently being given to a Professional Standards Board for Banking that would extend this approach and place greater emphasis on the membership of professional bodies.

PRINCIPLES AND ETHICS

Ethics are usually expressed in regulation in the form of principles. It is necessary for regulators and compliance practitioners to translate ethics and values into practice. This can be difficult, and the tools shown earlier help the process of translating *pure* ethics into actions, decisions, and behaviours, but it is easier to start from a more concrete and defined *principle* that incorporates the ethic into some more applied instruction or guidance. Regulators prefer to start from principles, as they are more tightly defined than ethics.

Listed in Table 4.1 are the Eleven Principles for Businesses of the UK's FCA, all of which are based to some degree on ethics.[4]

Regulators understand that ethics are broad ideas and need definition to implement but they also realise that using more principles in rule writing provides the basis for a more flexible approach to regulation, combining the ethical underpinning expected by society and the changing and varied needs of a large, international industry.

The value of principles is that they allow both compliance and regulators to make sensible and hopefully more sensitive and appropriate judgments. They allow for compliance to be more business-friendly cost-effective. Principles came to prominence when it became clear that simply increasing rules exponentially did not necessarily improve compliance outcomes. For example, the FSA Handbook, by 2007, occupied at least 9,500 pages and absorbed .5 percent of industry turnover. This was considered too much for an international centre to be competitive, and London saw principles-based regulation as one way of becoming more competitive, especially at a time when U.S. regulation was becoming more burdensome with approaches such as Sarbanes-Oxley.

TABLE 4.1 FCA's eleven principles for business.

1. Integrity	A firm must conduct its business with **integrity**.
2. Skill, care, and diligence	A firm must conduct its business with due skill, **care,** and diligence.
3. Management and control	A firm must take reasonable care to organise and control its affairs **responsibly** and effectively, with adequate risk management systems.
4. Financial prudence	A firm must maintain adequate financial resources.
5. Market conduct	A firm must observe **proper** standards of market conduct.
6. Customers' interests	A firm must pay due regard to the interests of its customers and treat them **fairly**.
7. Communications with clients	A firm must pay due regard to the information needs of its clients, and communicate information to them in a way which is **clear, fair, and not misleading.**
8. Conflicts of interest	A firm must manage conflicts of interest **fairly,** both between itself and its customers and between a customer and another client.
9. Customers: relationships of trust	A firm must take **reasonable care** to ensure the suitability of its advice and discretionary decisions for any customer who is entitled to rely upon its judgment.
10. Clients' assets	A firm must arrange adequate protection for clients' assets when it is **responsible** for them.
11. Relations with regulators	A firm must deal with its regulators in an **open and cooperative** way, and must disclose to the appropriate regulator anything relating to the firm of which that regulator would reasonably expect notice.

Note: Ethical terms or references are highlighted in **bold**. Principle 4 relates to prudence (in the title), which is an ethic.

On April 23, 2007, the FSA stated bluntly that "rules-based regulation had failed."[5] This represented a major turning point and launched an initiative to promote "more principles-based regulation" (MPBR). Broadly speaking, the move towards a more balanced approach has continued from this point and been taken up by many regulators worldwide. It is important to note that this change in direction came before the 2008 financial crisis and was a positive proactive move and not a response to 2008. Principles-based regulation was also not a cause of the GFC. The rules that failed in 2008 were essentially the capital adequacy rules, and these were quite prescriptive.

ADVANTAGES AND DISADVANTAGES OF PRINCIPLES

Table 4.2 sets out some of the advantages and some corresponding disadvantages.

TABLE 4.2 Positives and negatives of principles.

Positives	Negatives
■ Start with a purpose or rationale ■ Generally based on ethical principles or values ■ Lower cost; quicker and easier to write, consult on, and implement ■ Cover a wider range of possibilities—avoid gaps between rules ■ Few exceptions or need for qualifications ■ Little need for expensive legal advice or regulatory guidance—processes easier to engineer internally ■ Are generally "can do" ■ Outcomes driven: What is the point of this intervention? What result is it trying to create? ■ Easier to understand for nontechnical staff (i.e., noncompliance), empowering, embedding, and taking ownership at all levels ■ Encourage critical thinking, good judgment, and constructive challenge ■ Less need for technical training and board briefings ■ Enforcement easily understood by public, so more effective in PR and education terms ■ Can be seen as strong and progressive ■ Becoming more obviously used by regulators and as a basis for enforcement especially against senior staff ■ Raise status of compliance—seen as more judgment based, professional, and strategic ■ Can relate compliance to overall vision and values of the business and the sector ■ Social and stakeholder engagement facilitated ■ Clearer English, easier to understand	■ Purpose can sound very vague and may be difficult to express balance between consumer and market interests. ■ It is not always clear what ethics are being referred to and whether they are generally shared. ■ Can leave firms feeling confused and uncertain—this can lead to greater costs of compliance rather than less. ■ Not clear scope, leading to over-compliance or ignoring where relevant. ■ Greater need for expensive legal advice or regulatory guidance—regulator drawn into giving more written guidance. ■ Can lead supervision to become inconsistent—an uneven playing field—increasing cost and uncertainty. ■ Requests for clarity create need for regulator to issue explanations in informal speeches or "Dear-CEO" letters (which they may resist). ■ Outcomes are problematic for firms. Outcomes for whom, and how can they be measured? ■ Out of control for compliance as noncompliance staff make own interpretations. ■ Expensive in terms of staff training and board consultation. ■ Hard to supervise if interpretations differ from team to team. ■ Difficult for compliance to get resistant staff to take seriously. ■ Can be seen as weak and therefore unimportant—reduces effectiveness. ■ Enforcement can be more difficult as evidence harder to gather and prove in law; contributes to feeling of weakness. Considered by press, politicians, and public (and management?) as part of light-touch regulation, contributing to 2008 crises and thus discredited.

PRINCIPLES-BASED REGULATION

There are obviously both good and bad principles. Principles should not be confused with light-touch regulation (i.e., supervisory style, often blamed for contributing to the 2008 financial crisis). Principles, it should not be forgotten, are rules and very powerful enforcement tools. For a firm to have acted unfairly is usually adjudged to be deserving of a higher penalty than a technical breach of a specific process rule.

Good principles should:

- Be based on core ethics.
- Set out the purpose and intent of the rulemaking.
- Provide some sense of the desired outcomes.
- Define boundary conditions for unacceptable behaviour or standards.
- Point towards safe areas of compliance.

Principles-based regulation does not mean the absence of rules but a structure in which rules and guidance are based on principles and are only used when principles require further clarity.

The structure of the FSA and FCA/PRA rulebooks means that all elements are based on the 11 principles and the provenance of each set of rules and guidance is set out working its way back to one or more of these principles. There are similar principles for individuals. The clear structure does allow compliance and other users to connect the 11 principles to other parts of the FCA Handbook of rules and guidance as seen in Figure 4.3.

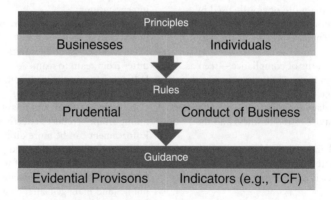

FIGURE 4.3 Compliance Structure

It is the regulators' skill—both in policy formulation and then in supervision and education—which determines how a constructive balance can be struck. This balance point may differ from sector to sector (it almost certainly will be more rules based in relation to securities), reflecting different risk profiles, and from time to time. As the development curve suggests, the balance will also evolve as the overall jurisdiction matures. This may be seen in the following case study.

CASE STUDY: Bribery Act—The Ultimate Principles-Based Regulation?

Context

This is a bold and sweeping ethical piece of principles-based lawmaking with wide-reaching implications. It is intended to tidy up existing laws but also place the UK in the forefront of anti-bribery legislation. The scope is wide, covering any public and business functions and activities and operating extraterritorially. This Act fits in with a range of other international laws, directives, and codes strengthening integrity and proper conduct in political and business life.

This Act is far reaching, aimed at enhancing free and fair competition and reducing the undermining effects of bribery. The scope is very wide. The Act applies to all UK companies and nationals, and overseas subsidiaries or associates, wherever they are operating, as well as any other companies operating in the UK. Companies must demonstrate that they have taken all practical steps to prevent bribery, in a risk-focused way, depending on their size, business, and complexity.

To paraphrase, the law basically says, "Do not do bribery; you know what it is." This is the principle and it needs only a small number of specifics, such as "Especially don't bribe public officials" and "Don't try the cultural excuse" (i.e., "That is how business is done around here").

Clearly, the law cannot use such straightforward language, so the offence is expressed as:

> The giving or accepting of financial or other advantage with the intention of inducing or rewarding "improper performance"—a failure of good faith, impartiality, or a position of trust.[6]

Then each term needs to be defined but the principle stays the same. The law feels obliged to spell out its scope and the test in general terms.

For example, the scope includes:

1. Offering or promising to give, and requesting or agreeing to receive
2. Giving or accepting when knowing or believing that acceptance of itself constitutes improper performance

3. Receiving on behalf of the person performing
4. Giving and receiving through third parties
5. In anticipation or in consequence
6. Functions and activities having no connection with the UK
7. Performed outside the UK
8. Actions omitted or not performed
9. Company of associated persons
10. Senior management of companies

The test is *relevant expectation:*

1. "What a reasonable person in the UK would expect"
2. If not performed in the UK—local written laws but not customs and practice
3. Published judicial decisions

While the law requires firms to have procedures in place to prevent bribery, good principles-based regulation will not prescribe what exactly compliance should do. However, from this principle it is surprising the range of actions that compliance could reasonably apply.

Here are some suggestions:

Communication and Leadership

1. The CEO and board will make a public commitment that "the company has a zero-tolerance of bribery."
2. The statement, accompanied by the final version of this policy document, is circulated to all staff and available on the company website.
3. Senior managers need to consider (i) whether to send copies to key stakeholders, suppliers, and counterparties and/or (ii) whether to include references in company documentation such as contract terms and conditions.
4. The commitment and policy will be reviewed by the board and reissued on an annual basis.

Training and HR

5. All staff will receive a briefing on the policy from their line management and/or compliance.
6. New staff will receive a briefing as part of their induction.
7. Staff can request guidance and clarification from compliance at any time.
8. Any updates or lessons learned will be integrated into existing Continuing Professional Development (CPD) cycles or if urgent circulated by compliance to all staff.
9. All job descriptions include a responsibility to implement the company's commitment and policy on combating bribery. The company policy will be made clear to all potential

applicants in writing and at interview. References will be checked for any indications of difficulties.

10. The normal disciplinary system applies on the basis that possible contravention of the Act and the company policy is a serious matter and potentially a criminal offence.

Monitoring and Due Diligence

11. The gifts, hospitality, and entertainments register—both given and received—will be extended to include:
    - The purpose of the gift
    - Whether the gift is related to any specific actual or potential contact or negotiation and the basic details of that contract
    - A declaration by the senior line manager involved or their successor one year on (frequency to be reviewed) that the gift, etc., did not have any connection to a specific contract, awarded or not

12. All substantial contracts or placement of business or due diligence will be accompanied by a new contracts register listing:
    - The criteria by which the contract or business was won or awarded
    - Those tendering and the terms of their bids (if awarding)
    - Any financial or other relationship between the company and individual staff members involved in awarding or obtaining the business and the outside party (if beyond normal business practise)
    - A record of anything of value given or received in obtaining the business or maintaining the contract

13. The CEO or senior manager may at any time terminate discussions, contacts, or business if the risk of bribery is considered sufficient.

14. Threshold levels for declarations and financial controls are to be set/reviewed annually by the board.

Reporting, Governance, and Whistleblowing

15. If there is any suspicion of bribery, any member of staff should contact their senior manager and the compliance officer using the same system as for suspicious transaction reporting for money laundering.

16. The compliance officer will report incidents to the CEO and the board immediately.

17. If for any reason staff or the compliance officer feel that their concerns cannot be reported in this way or that their concerns are not being treated seriously, they can contact the Non-Executive Director–Compliance. He will have a specific responsibility to review the systems and outcomes in this area. In exceptional circumstances it may be appropriate to use the company's whistleblowing system.

18. The gifts and contracts registers will be owned and reviewed by compliance on a rolling monthly basis, to consider trends emerging and their cost-effectiveness. The numbers of entries and any exceptions will be included in the monthly compliance report to the board. The records and registers will be held indefinitely.

Reviewing Systems and Risk Assessment

19. All senior managers must review their current operating procedures to ensure that there is no possibility that the company or staff are conducting business in a way that could be construed as being in contravention of the intentions or specifications of the Act or the company's policy. They must also assess the possible risks in their areas and specify particular interventions to address these. Departments must submit these risk plans to compliance annually. These declarations will be considered at the July board meeting, annually.
20. The risk committee will consider these reviews as part of the overall risk framework and include in the risk map.

Recordkeeping

21. The gifts, hospitality, and entertainments register—both given and received—will be extended to include:
    - The purpose of the gift
    - Whether the gift, etc., was related to any specific actual or potential contact or negotiation and the basic details of that contract
    - A declaration by the senior line manager involved or their successor one year on (frequency to be reviewed) that the gift, etc., did not have any connection to a specific contract, awarded or not

22. All substantial contracts or placement of business or due diligence will be accompanied by a new contracts register listing:
    - The criteria by which the contract or business was won or awarded
    - Those tendering and the terms of their bids (if awarding)
    - Any financial or other relationship between the company and individual staff members involved in awarding or obtaining the business and the outside party (if beyond normal business practise)
    - A record of anything of value given or received in obtaining the business or maintaining the contract

What Should Staff Do if They Have Any Suspicions?

23. If staff have any suspicions of bribery they should contact their senior manager and the compliance officer using the same system as for suspicious transaction reporting for money laundering.
24. The compliance officer will report incidents to the CEO and the board immediately.

25. If for any reason staff or the compliance officer feel that their concerns cannot be reported in this way or that their concerns are not being treated seriously, they can contact the Non-Executive Director–Compliance. He will have a specific responsibility to review the systems and outcomes in this area. In exceptional circumstances it may be appropriate to use the company's whistleblowing system.

26. The gifts and contracts registers will be owned and reviewed by compliance on a rolling monthly basis, to consider trends emerging and their cost-effectiveness. The numbers of entries and any exceptions will be included in the monthly compliance report to the board. The records and registers will be held indefinitely.

This example shows how from a few basic principles a whole set of policies and procedures can be established and implemented. These are not drawn from or validated by rules but are based on a compliance function drawing reasonable conclusions about what they see as appropriate for the scale, type, and nature of the business.

This is essentially about strengthening the core ethics of integrity, independence, and reliability. It leads on to a culture of anti-bribery, and culture is considered in the next chapter.

CONCLUSION

The success of principles also depends a great deal on the investment in compliance education that allows principles to be understood and valued. The active participation and support of compliance officers is:

- Within compliance departments
- Between compliance departments and the line and board
- Between compliance and regulators

If compliance staff push for more definition and fail to try to think for themselves, then principles-based regulation comes undone. More guidance is eventually forthcoming and the drift is back to interpreting in a black-and-white, tick-box fashion. It is essential that if efficiencies are to be realised, the development of principles-based regulation needs to be a shared effort, with compliance and regulators working in partnership. Investment in staff training is vital to ensure take-up and implementation. How principles are used has many consequences for compliance and the skills that compliance requires.

It is often missed that a major purpose of principles is to allow compliance differentiation and thereby greater product or service choice and competition. Compliance can be operated in many styles, from the conservative to creative. The firm risk-appetite statement is therefore crucial in articulating the approach selected. This is a conscious choice led by the board. The strength of understanding and confidence in using ethics determines the range of choices for compliance.

ENDNOTES

1. D. Jackman, *An Ethical Framework for Financial Services*, FSA Discussion Paper 18 (London: FSA, 2002).
2. Royal Bank of Scotland, *This Is Our Code* (Edinburgh: RBS, 2013), 5.
3. TC 1.1.4, *Financial Conduct Authority Handbook* (London: FCA, 2015).
4. Financial Conduct Authority, S2.1.1, *Principles for Businesses* (London: FCA, 2013).
5. FSA conference on the future of regulation 23.4.07.
6. UK Bribery Act 201p81 embed.

CHAPTER 5

Culture

One Team, One Dream.
　　—One of the "Forex fixing" team names revealed by FCA
　　　　　　　　　　　　　　　　　　　(November 13, 2014)

Ethics is not enough. Ethics and their associated principles need to be embedded and integrated into corporate culture.

For compliance to be effective and sustainable, especially under difficult conditions, ethics and principles need to be part of corporate culture and internalised in the hearts and minds of individuals. An emphasis on a culture has emerged as an essential element of regulation in two phases, one prior to the 2008 GFC, and one more recently. Using the UK and Singapore as the clearest examples of the two phases:

1. There is direct attention to influencing and measuring corporate culture, typified by the Treating Customers Fairly initiative in the UK starting in 2006–2007, and Fair Dealing in Singapore, introduced from 2010 within the Financial Advice Act.
2. The formation of FCA (UK's new Financial Conduct Authority) in 2013 brought a focus on *conduct risk*, defined as the likelihood of behaviours occurring that might produce poor consumer outcomes. This is an indirect approach to culture as behaviour arises from corporate culture. This second phase is also seen in Singapore with the Financial Advisory Industry Review (FAIR).

In a sense the second phase of interest in culture is a result of the first phase's perceived lack of success as many compliance departments failed to understand how to shape and influence culture. By reinventing the cultural focus in risk terminology this places culture firmly within the well-understood practices of risk management but at the same time diminishes the lead role of compliance. However, the indicators and techniques still hold good and are relevant. The FCA has not sought to revise the Treating Customers Fairly (TCF) guidance or supersede any of the principles involved and the MAS has not altered the outcomes established by both systems at the start.

As conduct risk arises from the behaviours associated with a less compliant culture, conduct risk and culture can be considered here as one and the same. One is a cause and the other is an effect. Culture *causes* conduct risk.

PRO-COMPLIANCE CULTURE

The embedding of corporate culture is a priority for compliance departments because a pro-compliance culture will deliver so many of the regulatory objectives, in theory, without too much intervention or cajoling by compliance. This allows compliance to become more advisory and strategic. This focus on culture is lower cost as it requires fewer compliance resources, should require less auditing and checking, and less time and effort is wasted on remediation and complaints. The development of a pro-compliance culture requires the empowering of everyone in the line and across the firm to buy into compliance objectives, to take individual and team responsibility, and to deliver the regulatory outcomes necessary and desirable. At its core is the philosophy that "prevention is better (and less costly) than cure."

Cultural change is a complex matter and requires the coordinated action of compliance, management, and the board (see Chapter 6). Each of the elements in the corporate structure and processes need to work together to influence and encourage certain behaviour and habits. This is a cumulative and cooperative process and underpins any concept of a *compliance revolution*.

The connection with ethics, values, and principles is clear; a firm needs to have an ethical culture in place or at least underway to understand and develop a pro-compliance culture since compliance and regulation is based on ethical values and principles. In the same way, regulators need to understand and emphasise ethics and be able to apply principles if they are to implement a cultural focus effectively and convincingly. It could be because this necessary condition was not fully in place in 2006–2007 that the first phase of UK cultural focus did not fully take hold or seem to be completely credible. Because it was unstable, the 2008 GFC swamped compliance efforts.

WHAT IS CULTURE?

Culture is the cumulation of the values, ethics, attitudes, habits, assumptions, heritage, expectations, and aspirations that shape everyday actions, decisions, and strategies. In any company, there are collective elements of culture embedded in the fabric of the company's "faith" (see Chapter 9). But no one is passive in this. Everyone's work is shaped by the corporate culture and also helps shape it—all staff are part of corporate culture and have a responsibility for it and what it delivers.

Culture can be said to exist within a company, the sector, and the industry as a whole. Some elements are local and others global, coming from accepted practices and centuries of interaction between financial centres and institutions. However, while some elements seem relatively stable, other elements of culture can change or be changed remarkably quickly.

WHAT IS A VALUES-LED MIND-SET?

A *mind-set* is a set of values or attitudes, as well as habits and practices, which impels people to act ethically and work towards good compliance outcomes. Mind-sets form a central part of the common, shared culture of the whole organisation. Changing culture needs a change in mind-set.

The key idea is that mind-sets are permanent or semi-fixed and so having a compliance mind-set provides a degree of confidence and assurance to the compliance team, the senior management, shareholders, and regulators that desirable compliance behaviours can be expected or are likely.

However, mind-sets develop over time and people understand their role more as well as the value and purposes of compliance and how to act ethically. So developing a compliance mind-set takes time and is akin to the wider learning experience. In fact it could be argued that an attitude of openness to new ideas and to learning is essential for a compliance mind-set to take root, to grow, and to be effective. Only by engaging in the process of learning will anyone become bought-in, committed, and engaged. Once engagement stops, other influences will emerge and the compliance mind-set will dissolve quickly. So constant work with influences on staff converging and support by the right kind of infrastructure is required to maintain a compliance mind-set.

Finally, compliance mind-sets are hard to measure and perhaps can be damaged by over-measurement. It is partly intuitive but also common sense. Culture is formed of many elements and is interconnected with internal and external factors as can be seen in Figure 5.1.

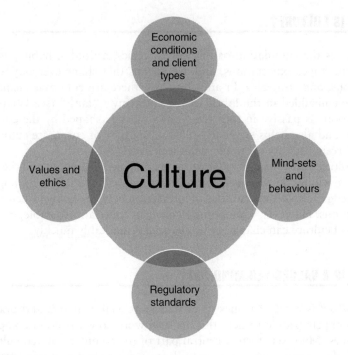

FIGURE 5.1 Aspects of Corporate Culture

CHANGING AND EMBEDDING CULTURE

Culture may change from within as, for example, new management arrives, or from compliance initiatives, or as a result of external factors such as public or client pressure, changing economic circumstances, crises, and/or government policies. Internal and external factors working together usually are highly effective in shaping and reshaping corporate culture.

If you can alter culture, even slightly, you will by definition affect the way everything is done subsequently in the company, the decisions at every level, and the outcomes of the company and sector. This is why culture is of such interest to regulators and compliance. If you can change culture, you are addressing the *causes* of problems and opportunities, not the symptoms (e.g., firefighting, regulatory breaches, or systems failures). Cleaning up failures is messy and costly for any firm, for compliance and the regulators, so this approach of shaping a culture saves costs.

Culture is also key to managing reputation. It is possible to develop a reputational advantage from a sound ethical culture—for example, Standard Chartered's "Here for Good" campaign in Singapore.

"Here for Good" is made up of three pillars:

1. To Be Here for people
2. To Be Here for progress (We do the right thing—a force for good, making a positive contribution to the economies and societies in which we operate)
3. To Be Here for the long run

The brand comes alive in the behaviour and values we show. We do our best to be:

1. Courageous
2. Responsive
3. International
4. Creative
5. Trustworthy[1]

A firm that demonstrates a good standard of ethical culture can attract better staff and will generate loyalty internally. For compliance, an ethical corporate culture throughout its business dealings can significantly raise staff awareness of compliance issues, which in turn can lead to early identification of problems and generate cost and reputation savings for the firm.

Corporate Culture Failings

There have been severe failures brought about by culture that is not supportive of compliance. Regulators have been asking themselves why poor decisions are made and problems are allowed to happen in the first place, and in some cases it is the entire culture of the firm. Detailed reports into individual failings of banks (RBS, HBOS, Barclays, etc.) show that these values are transmitted within the culture of a firm and not prevented by poor governance structures and practices. Sir David Walker, in his report on corporate governance failings following 2008, stated that these failings were more a matter of behaviours and culture than of organisational failings.[2] This view is supported by the following case reports:

Case 1: RBS Report by FSA[3]

Para 575

Some aspects of management, governance and culture can be assessed fairly precisely. For example, it is possible to identify whether a bank has appropriate formal processes of governance by reviewing matters such as whether board agendas cover appropriate issues and management information flows to the appropriate level. However, many of the important questions about management, governance and culture cover issues such as boardroom dynamics, management style and shared values. These, by their nature, are matters of judgement and are difficult to assess precisely, even on the basis of contemporaneous documentation. For example, assessing whether key board decisions were subject to adequate monitoring and challenge is inherently difficult, as the minutes of board meetings typically record the decisions taken rather than the detail of how or why a particular decision was arrived at, or whether alternative views were expressed in the course of the debate. And assessing a firm's culture effectively is difficult even when done contemporaneously, let alone when attempting to assess the past. Despite these difficulties, the Review Team has concluded that it is highly probable that aspects of RBS's management, governance and culture played a role in the story of RBS's failure and should be addressed in this Report.

Para 663

The crucial cultural questions relevant to RBS's failure, however, relate not to the fair treatment of customers, but to whether RBS was over-confident about its abilities, had too optimistic an outlook, and was too focused on revenue and profit at the expense of balance sheet risk. In each of the three ARROW reviews during the Review Period, the Supervision Team identified significant growth in RBS's business, and was rightly concerned that this might not be balanced by a recognition that control systems needed to keep pace.

Case 2: House of Lords/House of Commons Parliamentary Commission on Banking Standards

"An Accident Waiting to Happen": The Failure of HBOS 2012–2013[4]

The strategy set by the Board from the creation of the new Group sowed the seeds of its destruction. HBOS set a strategy for aggressive, asset-led growth across divisions over a sustained period. This involved accepting more risk across all divisions of the Group. Although many of the strengths of the two brands within HBOS largely persisted at branch level, the strategy created a new culture in the higher echelons of the bank. This culture was brash, underpinned by a belief that the growing market share was due to a special set of skills which HBOS possessed and which its competitors lacked. The effects of the culture were all the more corrosive when coupled with a lack of corporate self-knowledge at the top of the organisation, enabling the bank's leaders to persist in the belief, in some cases to this day, that HBOS was a conservative institution when in fact it was the very opposite.

Case 3: Barclays' Saltz Review[5]

Banks in particular are built on trust. After all, they look after our money. Banking requires that we have trust and confidence that our bank is not taking undue risk. Building an organisation's reputation for trustworthiness takes time and is founded on a robust ethical culture supported by leaders, systems and policies designed to foster and reinforce employee trustworthiness. In industries that are associated with risk and risk-taking, the work that must be done to establish and sustain trust is greater. Barclays' work on culture and values comes at a time when trust in banking and bankers is at an all-time low. Trust comes from an expectation that what is said will be delivered. Trust is also strongly related to fairness. Studies show that the experience of unfairness quickly erodes trust.

… Values drive everyday behaviour, helping to define what is normal and acceptable, explaining how things ought to be (for example, staff ought to put customers first). Values provide a framework through which the natural and often difficult conflicts that arise in people's day-to-day work can be resolved. But they will not always provide the answers. Organisations need to create an environment where employees feel it is safe to resolve the frequent differences that arise. For example, on a daily basis, retail bank staff can face the dilemma of determining which deposit product best meets customer needs given the frequency with which interest rates and conditions can change.

… [T]here is a significant challenge to instilling shared values in a universal bank like Barclays. Cultural compatibility is difficult to achieve across businesses which may attract very different employee profiles, and where the business model and objectives are different. It takes a great deal of finesse to translate the same common values into credible expectations of a trading floor and of a retail branch network. This task is made harder when, as at Barclays, rapid growth (which propelled it from a family bank to a leading universal bank), multiple reorganisations and extensive external hiring (particularly in the investment bank) create a less stable cultural base.

… Our review of the performance evaluation documentation revealed little emphasis on culture and values. Where present, there was little evidence of how the performance evaluation process used values effectively as a means to drive behaviour. For example, in the investment bank, although "integrity" was specified to be a key value, the performance evaluation parameters used to determine integrity (even in relative terms) were ill-defined. The crux to embedding values is as much about the zero-tolerance for value breaches as it is about determining what good looks like. Some of the failures to report and escalate poor behaviours relating to the LIBOR issues demonstrate quite how loosely certain values were applied.

HOW TO CHANGE CULTURE

We have developed the concept of *crucibles* as frameworks that provide the necessary structure for cultural change. What compliance needs to do is to construct these crucibles within a firm and manage them. The concept of the crucible brings into play the twin elements of freedom/empowerment of staff within a pressured and pro-scribed container.

Crucibles and Judgment-Based Compliance

We are proposing that there needs to be more crucibles—opportunities and structures for cultural change and constructive challenge. These should be built so that they contain everyday situations and processes, in business, that explicitly and directly encourage individual and collective questioning and quality deliberation, within carefully risk-controlled boundaries. This is a new science and sometimes an art.

The parts of the crucible are shown in Figure 5.2:

1. *Creating strong boundaries*: The walls of the crucible need to be robust and are constructed of "solid and secure blocks" such as board vision, direction, and standards (the lid), firm values and ethics (the base), appraisal, reward, and sanction policies (side 1), and policies and procedures based on principles that provide clear boundaries for unacceptable behaviour (side 2).

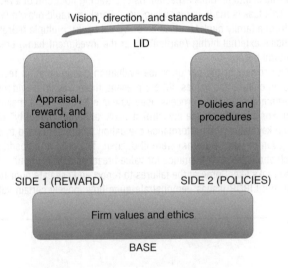

FIGURE 5.2 Composition of Crucible

2. *Allowing insight and empowerment*: The space within the crucible allows for individuals and teams to look for suitable input and consider options while being empowered to make their own decisions, which they can then own and be accountable for. This requires prescription to be removed or relaxed over time so that predetermined "right" answers are not always available. Without removing these rote answers and box ticking staff will not mature and gain a sense of responsibility.

   This increase of people risk is the only way of reducing people and conduct risk long term. Mistakes will be made but these are essential for learning and the reward and sanction implications must be sensitively and appropriately handled (not too heavy-handed, yet meaningful).

3. *"Heating"*: Applying heat to this mixture in the crucible can consist of constructive challenge mechanisms together with communication of positive and negative cases, and continual training and education, including the logging of learning, and leadership that walks the talk both internally and externally.

   It is not about precooked solutions; there must not be set cultural norms overly defined, or the creativeness of the process is lost. Even worse is a system of nudging, coaxing staff towards solutions or decisions, which would appear in a crucible process as deceitful and corrosive. This is about opening debate to all and empowering absolutely everyone in everyday situations, making decisions, dealing with a complaint, setting a strategy, and mending a problem effectively and for the long term.

4. *"Plighting"* to a set of ethics, values, and principles and basing your decisions and actions on these needs above all, requires trust. It needs trust in senior management that they will see actions and any mistakes in their proper context, and that regulators will also trust good intent and a sound crucible process.

Making and using crucibles is essentially a collective experience. It is not IQ dependent, it does not need or feed circles of exclusivity and power, and in its best form, it does not need acceding, rights, or accreditation. It is open to robust challenge and debate—it is about giving room to form good judgments. We have seen that good process is never a substitute for good judgment.

Crucibles create an environment where difficult issues and questions are raised regularly so that they become part of everyday normal conversation and culture. Everyone will build confidence and competence in handling these issues and it will be clearer what you define as being acceptable or not. The decision-making process can also be visualised as a funnel in and out of a decision space as in Figure 5.3.

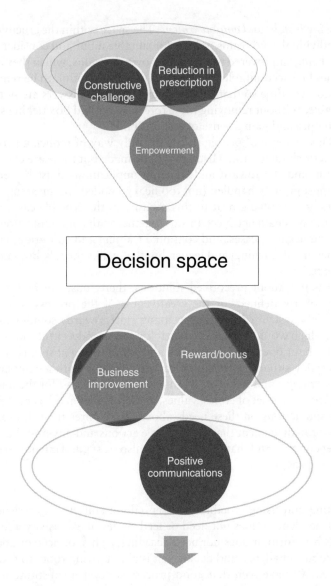

FIGURE 5.3 Composition of Decision Making

Obviously it is a learning process and sometimes there will be a number of "right answers" or no apparent straightforward answer. Sound leadership may well be required to find the best fit and precedents may be useful.

Regulation reduces the need to think and to engage. A large rulebook of right answers suggests that just looking up the right answer in the right place is enough. But it is not. It leads to box-ticking and black-and-white decisions: "Just tell me whether I can do it." There is no understanding, no long-term embedding or education. So regulatory evolution is vital for this cultural maturity to happen. Rules need to be balanced with principles and recognition needs to be given to mature culture or good intent to move towards values-led culture.

CREATING CRUCIBLES IN REGULATION—EXAMPLES

In the same way crucibles can be created to drive change inside businesses, crucible structures can be inserted inside regulatory instruments to drive change across an industry. Crucially they should focus attention on principles and direction (or intent) and put the pressure on users to make their own decisions within that permissible space. Here are some examples of how this new style of rule writing has consciously been trialed.

FSA/FCA Training and Competence Requirements

Training and competence rules started in securities regulation in the 1980s, first in the United States with a series of compulsory registration examinations, and then it followed in the UK after 1986 with similar Registered Representative exams that allowed access to the registers of key traders and dealers. The aim was to set a standard for market participation that would protect market efficiency and stop unskilled traders and brokers from operating inefficiently or costing firms and in some circumstances clients unnecessarily.

The securities regimes remained relatively simplistic with a pass/fail entry exam, although the London Stock Exchange added diploma qualification for Exchange membership (and therefore partnership in stockbroking firms). However, the concept was extended in the investment and advice sectors after the publication by SIB of Oonagh MacDonald's report, which highlighted deficiencies in investment advice, especially by untrained advisors in the pensions industry.

The aim now was more acutely consumer protection and it became a major tool in combating widespread mis-selling in the 1990s. Special exams were created by a range of institutes and training became much more common in sectors where previously there had been only superficial investment in education. The regime became compulsory in 1996, with the grandfathering provisions (allowing for experienced practitioners) ended. Many thousands who could not qualify left the industry, some going abroad, and enforcement was rigorous, imposing selling restrictions on any firm without suitably trained sales forces.

In 1996–1998, IMRO extended the regime to administration functions, targeting supervisors, to try to improve error rates. Rules covered by then the processes of recruitment, induction, training, assessment, examination, record keeping, supervision, and maintaining CPD (continuing professional development).

Training and competence had a heritage of detailed, prescriptive rules that set out exactly what firms had to do to ensure competent staff and how to demonstrate competence. The rules from SROs inherited by FSA focused on establishing systems and controls that would deliver and maintain competent staff and not on why they should be competent (outcome) or what it meant to be competent (beyond controlling exam syllabi). These rules were very expensive to follow and required specialist compliance staff or functions both in firms and also in the regulators. Firms did not have to work out much for themselves and the regulators provided layers of guidance and expert advice, often through regional roadshows. The cumulative volume of regulation was substantial and increasingly counterproductive.

FSA inherited some 500 pages of such rules and guidance in 1998. In 2000, it consulted in CP34 on a principles-led approach, the first of its kind at FSA.

This had two components:

1. Commitments setting out the high-level outcomes of Training and Competence (although still in fairly process forms)[6]

Commitments—as Originally Drafted (no longer part of rulebook):

- Advance and maintain the competence of its employees.
- Ensure that its employees remain competent for the functions they carry out.
- Ensure that its employees are adequately supervised in relation to the attainment and maintenance of competence.
- Ensure that the training for and competence of its employees is regularly reviewed.
- In dealing with commitments (1)–(4), take account of the level of competence that is necessary having regard to the nature of its business and the role of its employees.

These commitments are specific principles based on FCA Principle 3 and also have some element of outcome expressed within them (see Chapter 7).

2. On these specific principles are hung *detailed rules* where deemed necessary to get over a specific point, for example, the need to pass an exam before operating unsupervised:

e.g. TC

> A firm must not assess an employee as competent to carry on an activity in TC Appendix 1 until the employee has demonstrated the necessary competence to do so and has (if required by TC Appendix 1) attained each module of an appropriate qualification. This assessment need not take place before the employee starts to carry on the activity.
>
> A firm may assess an employee who is subject to, but has not satisfied, an appropriate qualification requirement as competent. To an extent the level of guidance and regulatory advice was cut right down so that firms had to think for themselves. Only a recognised exam list remained which was in 2004 moved to be managed by the newly formed Financial Services Skills Council—FSSC—as part of a move to increase the level of ownership of the industry of this basic area which it was very much in their interests to develop. In many cases firms benefitted form being super-equivalent.[7]

This was effectively creating a crucible in the rules and thereby a crucible in every regulated firm. This was the intention to enable firms to take control of this area of previously intensive and costly regulation in a way that could benefit the business and also secure the consumer protection essentials as, for example, in Figure 5.4.

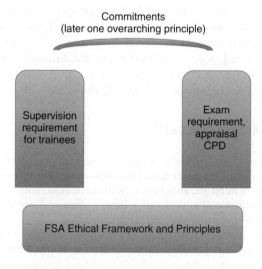

FIGURE 5.4 Crucible in Practice

Note: The introduction of MiFID in the mid-2000s reduced the commitments to one overarching principle, which lost some of the granularity:

- High level rule—MiFID Article 5.1(d)
    A firm must employ personnel with the skills, knowledge and expertise necessary . . . .[8]

Ethics was added specifically in the FSA's definition of expertise in TC 1.1.4 01/11/2007:

> . . . competence means having the skills, knowledge and expertise needed to discharge the responsibilities of an employee's role. This includes achieving a good standard of ethical behaviour.[9]

These formulations have seemed to be popular with firms and deliver better compliance results, in less costly ways. Further trimmings of the rules base proved to be going too far, requiring firms to ask many more questions, and so were reversed.

REGULATORY METHODOLOGIES

This shift of emphasis to examining corporate culture and the internal drivers or causes of undesirable behaviour has led to new forms of regulation methodology internationally. The most concerted early direct approach to culture has been in the FSA and FCA's approach to Treating Customers Fairly—a term directly related to the core ethics identified in FSA DP 18 in 2002.[10] A similar strategy has been developed in Singapore around the "Fair Dealing" Guidance, an addendum to the Financial Advisers Act.[11] This approach has been continued as part of the conduct risk agenda, as the following extracts from an FCA speech show.

How does FCA Assess Culture?[12]

> Regulators have begun to make explicit statements about culture and ethics. Supervision and enforcement action has increasingly been based on corporate culture and mind-set. However, regulators are reluctant to spell out culture in hard measures but prefer to indicate culture and mind-sets through the combination of many statements and measures.
>
> When FCA started it said: It is only through establishing the right culture that senior management can convert their good intentions into actual

fair outcomes for consumers and ensure that delivery of [regulatory] outcomes is sustainable.

This is very different from what we have today where the focus has been on ensuring compliance with a set of rules rather than doing the right thing for customers. Looked at this way, the responsibility for ensuring the right outcomes for customers resides with everyone at the firm, led by senior management, and not as something delegated to compliance or control functions.

The challenge for many firms is that culture is hard to change and requires dedicated and persistent focus over a number of years in order to embed different approaches and ways of behaving. As the Saltz Review recently concluded, if culture is left to its own devices, it shapes itself, with the inherent risk that behaviours will not be those desired.

Drivers of culture at a firm:

1. Setting the tone from the top

   Setting the tone is all about creating a culture where everyone has ownership and responsibility for doing the right thing, because it is the right thing to do. It is about setting values and translating them into behaviours. This can only be established by the CEO and other members of the senior management team, who need to not only set out the key company values, but also personally demonstrate they mean them through their actions.

2. Business practices and ways of behaving

   The task then is to translate this tone into business practices that drive how business decisions are made, how the firm responds to events, how individuals should behave and how issues are elevated in an open way. For me, therefore, translating culture into business practices is a way to make culture into something more hard edged.

3. Performance management, employee development, and reward programmes

   Performance management, employee development and reward programmes are clearly a powerful lever to influence the culture of any organisation. We have seen in financial services how the misalignment between incentives structures and corporate values has led to significant damage.

The FCA Assesses Culture by "Joining the Dots"

Our approach today is to draw conclusions about culture from what we observe about a firm—in other words, joining the dots rather than assessing culture directly. This can be through a range of different measures such as how a firm responds to, and deals with, regulatory issues; what customers are actually experiencing when they buy a product or service from front-line staff; how a firm runs its product approval process and the considerations around these; the manner in which decisions are made or escalated; the behaviour of that firm on certain markets; and even the remuneration structures.

We also look at how a board engages in those issues, including whether it probes high return products or business lines, and whether it understands strategies for cross-selling products, how fast growth is obtained and whether products are being sold to markets they are designed for.

We are able, from all of this, to draw conclusions about the culture of a firm. This includes assessing if the perceived customer-focused culture is supported by, for example, regular discussions on conduct at board level and appropriate sales incentives plans.

How Will the FCA Encourage Positive Culture Change in Firms?

We don't have direct rules about culture, although our high-level principles for business come close to this in some respects. As I have set out here, we don't directly supervise "culture." However, as culture and business practices are so important in driving behaviours, we do want to encourage positive culture change in firms.

TCF Case Study

This was the first determined attempt to introduce culturally focused regulation. The principles were defined in Singapore just as in the UK.

The five fair dealing outcomes in Singapore are:

Outcome 1: Customers have confidence that they deal with financial institutions where fair dealing is central to the corporate culture.

Outcome 2: Financial institutions offer products and services that are suitable for their target customer segments.

Outcome 3: Financial institutions have competent representatives who provide customers with quality advice and appropriate recommendations.

Outcome 4: Customers receive clear, relevant, and timely information to make informed financial decisions.

Outcome 5: Financial institutions handle customer complaints in an independent, effective, and prompt manner.

The UK has an outcome:

Consumers do not face unreasonable post-sale barriers imposed by firms to change product, switch provider, submit a claim, or make a complaint.

UK INDICATORS

In the UK this was supported by a framework of controls on which firms were expected to focus.

Key Cultural Drivers:

- Leadership
- Strategy
- Decision making
- Controls
- Recruitment
- Training and competence
- Reward

The key aim was not to tell firms what to do, but for them to work it out for themselves. Therefore, no specific new rule-writing emerged but instead a series of questions for a firm to ask. The key issue is *embedding*:

> While most senior management in firms can explain what treating customers fairly means to them and how this is reflected within the firm's strategy, middle management are often failing to deliver fair consumer outcomes within their business areas. We believe this is often due to senior management not giving middle management enough direction, and also failing to monitor them.
>
> Many of the examples of poor practice we have seen relate to an unreasonable expectation by senior management of middle management's ability to deliver fair consumer outcomes given the structure, pressures and incentives that they face.
>
> They also reflect failure by senior management and middle management to adequately monitor the delivery of good TCF behaviour and fair consumer outcomes. Where middle management feels empowered by senior management, both within their role and in their ability to challenge policies and procedures, there is less risk of unfair consumer outcomes.[13]

And

> Strategies, policies or procedures that deliver unfair consumer outcomes are not always challenged. We have identified firms where the senior management of a business unit or firm have not challenged a strategy that conflicts with TCF, for instance where it has been set by a parent company. This is often because of a fear that speaking up against an inappropriate strategy could have implications for the individual's remuneration or employment. In other situations, policies or procedures have not received

enough challenge, as there was either not a formal process in place or the environment was not conducive to challenge by staff or customers.[14]

The TCF initiative involved many cultural shifts, such as:

1. Openness to new ideas and strategic leadership demonstrably driving for fair treatment of customers.
2. Understanding that business and regulatory outcomes can converge successfully.
3. Willingness to listen to staff and customers (supported by measures to capture feedback and experiences).
4. Understanding that fair treatment doesn't necessarily equal satisfactory treatment.
5. Driving implementation of stress-testing products and processes.
6. A willingness and ability to raise concern if products/markets/processes are becoming overly complex.
7. Incorporate TCF within regulatory risk assessment.
8. Ensure processes remain separate from outcomes.
9. Ensure measurements have tolerance or triggers to ensure intervention as appropriate.
10. Risk assessments are to be reviewed and adjusted according to market, business, and regulatory developments.
11. Internal audit and compliance monitoring programmes to incorporate TCF points.
12. Encourage staff and consumer feedback; ensure feedback is listened to, assessed, and action taken where appropriate.
13. Establish ongoing communication and awareness programmes for employees.
14. Ensure the delivery of fair outcomes is incorporated into all staff goals and objectives—from CEO to frontline staff.
15. Remuneration plans to actively encourage staff behaviours consistent with TCF.
16. Don't just measure customer satisfaction.

The TCF initiative was initially poorly understood and the following issues were often identified and lessons were learned.

Leadership:

1. Senior management do not actively seek to readdress the prevailing culture.
2. Rewards and incentives do not allow TCF behaviours to be embedded.
3. Senior managers do not play an active role in directing the TCF strategy.

Business Strategy:

1. Business strategies do not have recourse to the effect/impact on customers.
2. Business strategies focus on growth without consideration of quality of growth.

Advice Process:

1. Overly complex and unclear suitability letters.
2. Firms do not challenge providers robustly regarding products and services.
3. Advisor Training and Competence (T&C) scheme not robust to cover complex product propositions.

Post-Advice:

1. MI measures business process rather than TCF outcomes.
2. Complaints are not subject to FCA referral.
3. Rewards are made despite poor/inadequate advice having been given.
4. Action is not taken when MI indicates poor treatment of customers.
5. Staff and employee feedback are not routinely collected and analysed together with action plans.
6. Placing reliance on customer satisfaction as a measure of TCF.

In 2007, FSA set out examples of good practice. Here is one set of examples:

Example 1:

- **Controls**—In general, firms are finding it hard to identify, collect, interpret and use relevant MI to monitor TCF effectively and to demonstrate they are treating their customers fairly. Even when appropriate MI is collected, many firms do not undertake qualitative analysis or provide effective commentary for those within the firm that receive the information.

    Good practice—controls

- **Checking staff understand and implement TCF**—One firm completes quarterly "knowledge health checks" in the form of 30-minute interviews with randomly selected members of staff to check they understand and apply key issues correctly. A report is produced for senior management and middle management, which summarises the interviews and suggests corrective action where a weakness in the approach has been identified. This shows the firm checks understanding and implementation and considers this to be useful MI to support delivery of fair consumer outcomes.

- **Monitoring delivery of fair consumer outcomes**—In one firm, all members of the management team from CEO to Team Leaders listen to two hours of randomly selected call centre calls. They then give the staff involved immediate constructive feedback. This is a useful control and the information gathered could be used to show the firm is checking consumer outcomes and correcting poor behaviour.
- **Checking TCF behaviour and feedback**—One firm used a hidden camera "mystery shopping" exercise to monitor front-line staff and to identify examples of good and bad practice. Staff watched the results online or on DVD which included an accompanying commentary by senior management. The "learning" points identified during this exercise and the process for feeding this back to staff appeared effective in influencing staff.

Poor practice—controls

- **Confusing the customer**—In many firms, controls are focused on delivering information but do not give enough consideration to customer understanding. In one firm, we identified a strong controls culture, which ensured that call centre staff provided the customer with all the facts about a product. But in one call, a very large amount of this information was simply read out without any break, and it was clear that the customer had "switched off" during the conversation. Where a firm discloses a lot of important information over the phone, it may wish to consider ways it could retain the customer's attention throughout the conversation.
- **Limited qualitative data**—We have identified that firms' MI is often limited to quantitative data, which is sometimes very narrow in scope, and is often not supported with qualitative data. In a number of firms, we have seen MI on the products being sold and the commission received, but minimal information on the quality of the sale made. Firms might wish to consider how best to monitor the quality of sales. Appropriate measures vary. In an advised environment, it might be relevant to look at incidence of advice without a (commission earning) product sale, as well as execution only or insistent customer business. For products with high upfront costs, persistency is of interest. Data on refused claims or complaints can also be informative. This will enable a firm to monitor the competence of the adviser and the quality of their sales. This information could also be reflected in the assessment of the competence of the adviser. It may also be useful in reaching a conclusion over the validity of a customer complaint as part of any investigation where the suitability of the advice is being questioned.

- **Ineffective controls**—We have identified ineffective controls in some firms. One firm monitored the number of investment trades to identify potential "churning." However, the firm did not use this information to investigate potentially poor sales, but instead it wrote to the client to ask if they were satisfied with the advice. This is not enough on the quality of the sale as the client may not realise that they have been subject to churning. It is important where MI is collected that appropriate action is taken to ensure that the risks to consumers are minimised.

- **Not enough focus by senior management**—One firm had structured their TCF programme around their processes and delegated responsibility for their action plans to managers owning the processes. A significant amount of activity had taken place but the MI was not focused enough to enable senior management to monitor progress and explain if the actions mitigate their key TCF risks. For example, the CEO could not tell how the firm would factor TCF into key decisions, or whether they had made any progress in two significant areas for the firm. The firm has now re-started a "top down" gap analysis, with each key risk and action plan owned by a senior executive.

- **Not enough MI**—A number of firms have failed adequately to monitor their advisers. They did not collect data on the number of instances, either on an individual or group basis, where they were delivering unfair consumer outcomes. One firm did not take corrective action when this occurred.

- **Failing to collect MI**—One firm had not developed controls to capture and monitor customer feedback received by the call centre. This meant the firm was unable to identify where they had failed to meet their own internal service standards, or how it could be improved.[15]

CASE STUDY: Enforcement

FSA issues ban and fine of £500,000 against former HBOS executive, Peter Cummings:*

The Financial Services Authority (FSA) has fined Peter Cummings £500,000 and banned him from holding any senior position in a UK bank, building society, investment or insurance firm. This is the highest fine imposed by the FSA on a senior executive for management failings.

The FSA's action relates to the period between January 2006 and December 2008, during which time Cummings was an executive director of HBOS plc and chief executive of its Corporate Division.

Under Cummings' direction, the division pursued an aggressive growth strategy, despite these known weaknesses in the control framework. This focus on growth peaked in 2007 and continued into 2008, despite Cummings being aware

---

*FSA/PN/087/2012 (Sept. 12, 2012).

of concerns within HBOS about some of the markets in which the division operated and growing signs of problems in the economy. Rather than taking reasonable steps to mitigate potential risks, he directed his division to increase its market share as other lenders were pulling out of deals.

Cummings led a culture of optimism that also affected the division's judgement about bad debts. The division did not adequately monitor the deterioration of high value transactions and was slow to pass them to the dedicated "High Risk and Impaired Assets" team for more detailed assessment of the likelihood of default and the corresponding level of provision that should be raised.

The assessment of individual provisions was consistently optimistic rather than prudent and Cummings chose not to follow the approach to levels of provisioning which had been suggested by HBOS's auditors and the division's own Risk function.

... the FSA has judged Cummings to be personally culpable in breaching Statement of Principle 6 of the FSA's Code of Practice for Approved Persons, by failing to exercise due skill, care and diligence in managing HBOS's Corporate Division during this critical period.

Tracey McDermott, director of enforcement and financial crime, said:

Despite being aware of the weaknesses in his division and growing problems in the economy, Cummings presided over a culture of aggressive growth without the controls in place to manage the risks associated with that strategy. Instead of reacting to the worsening environment, he raised his targets as other banks pulled out of the same markets.

It is essential that senior executives understand that incentivising revenue over risk is a dangerous folly. Growth is a sound ambition for any business but risk must be properly managed and robust controls are imperative to ensure growth is achieved in a way that is both stable and sustainable.[16]

FAIR DEALING IN SINGAPORE

The FAA Fair Dealing Guidelines 2010 and the recent Financial Advisory Industry Review (FAIR) proposals of 2013 are a perfect example of these methods.

The FAIR aims:

(a) Raising the competence of FA representatives;
(b) Raising the quality of FA firms;
(c) Making financial advising a dedicated service;
(d) Lowering distribution costs; and
(e) Promoting a culture of fair dealing.
    The questions Boards and Senior Management should ask
      1.6.1 How do the Board and Senior Management lead the financial institution in delivering the fair dealing outcomes to its customers? Are executive responsibilities clearly assigned?

    1.6.2 Have the Board and Senior Management reviewed the financial institution's business model to ensure that it supports fair dealing with its customers? How is the achievement of the fair dealing outcomes incorporated into the financial institution's policies and practices?

    1.6.3 How do the Board and Senior Management clearly communicate to internal and external stakeholders the message that delivering the fair dealing outcomes is a priority for the financial institution?

    1.6.4 How do the Board and Senior Management measure and monitor the achievement of the fair dealing outcomes? What measures have the Board and Senior Management drawn up to address areas where the financial institution as fallen short of delivering the fair dealing outcomes?

The recent introduction of a Balanced Scorecard (BSC) framework is to promote good behaviour and to encourage representatives to provide quality advice and suitable recommendations. Quality of advice and suitability of recommendations are thus the important drivers of a representative's remuneration, rather than sales volume. As remuneration drives behaviour, a significant proportion of an FA representative's remuneration should be based on the representative's performance on the non-sales KPIs. As supervisors have influence and responsibility over how their representatives conduct their FA activities, they should be remunerated according to the performance of their representatives under the BSC framework.

MAS proposed four non-sales KPIs in the BSC framework, covering the following areas:

1. Understanding customers' needs
2. Suitability of product recommendations
3. Adequacy of information disclosure
4. Standards of professionalism and ethical conduct

MEASURING CULTURE

There are several ways of measuring culture and conduct risk. The first emanates from the TCF regime and identifies positive and negative indicators of pro-compliance and noncompliant culture. Some extracts are provided in Table 5.1.

Second, it is possible to consider outcomes of values-led mature compliance culture versus mechanical, unsophisticated compliance. The addition of numerical measures is developed in Chapter 7 where the question of what exactly outcomes are desirable comes to the fore in stage 5 of the General Model.

Some examples are given in Table 5.2.

TABLE 5.1 Positive and negative indicators of compliance culture.

Positive Behaviours	Decision Making	Negative Behaviours
Where decisions are taken that affect customers, the decision maker always gathers the relevant information. This includes feedback from customers and staff where this will help ensure a fair outcome for customers.	Informed	Unfair decisions are taken because insufficient information has been gathered. Decision makers do not consider or investigate relevant feedback from staff or customers.
Individuals have the relevant skills and expertise to enable them to take a decision that affects customers. Where applicable they recognise they do not have sufficient understanding; they have access to expert guidance. They understand the need for decisions to take account of the interests of different customer groups and shareholders.	Competent	Decision makers lack the necessary skills or expertise and are unwilling or unable to seek advice. They generally favour shareholders' interests over those of the customer.
Individuals have the confidence and authority to take the decisions required of their role and understand when they need to escalate the decision. This includes circumstances where a flexible approach provides a fairer result for a customer	Empowered	Individuals lack confidence or misunderstand their authority, leading them to be indecisive or make unfair decisions (e.g., a failure to recognise an individual customer's circumstances).
Management have created a culture where staff can challenge decisions made about customer issues. The firm recognises challenge from customers and acts on this when it is fair to do so.	Open to challenge	Staff members do not feel they can challenge decisions that they think are not fair to customers. There are inadequate mechanisms to allow challenges from customers. Challenges from customers are dismissed without consideration.
The firm records decisions about customer issues, including the rationale for what was decided. It maintains these for an appropriate length of time. The records can be accessed easily when required.	Recorded	There are poor or incomplete records of decisions about customer issues that cannot be retrieved easily or at all.

TABLE 5.2 Ethical and compliant outcomes.

Example Issue	Ethical Outcomes	Compliant Outcomes
Complaints	▪ Complaints responded to in 24 hours with an indication of next steps and possible outcomes, preferably in a nonstandardised format. ▪ Clients see complaint is valued, being dealt with as quickly as possible—less likely to pass on their dissatisfaction. ▪ May strengthen relationship with client and improve business.	▪ Initial response as promptly as FSA rules require—minimum information in standard format. Customers can be distanced and feel disenfranchised. ▪ More likely to pass on dissatisfaction to others so reputational damage is greater. ▪ The client may switch firms in the long term or reduce business.
Marketing	▪ No small print used as this obscures information. Key information spelt out in plain English. ▪ No disclaimers used, unless absolutely necessary. ▪ Customers less likely to be mis-sold, especially in more vulnerable groups. Regulatory benefit. ▪ Customers behave more responsibly and with greater understanding if they need further explanations.	▪ Font sizes as permitted by FCA. All possible non-sales information relegated to back pages and small text in legalese. ▪ All disclaimers on all communications. ▪ More opportunity for confusion and thereby mis-selling and reputational/regulatory loss. ▪ Consumers may be more likely to dispute terms and conditions or feel dissatisfied if claims and expectations (which may be unrealistic) are not met.
Product design	▪ Designing products that deliver sustainable results, if not spectacular, and are available on an even playing field for existing and new customers, provides customers with the reassurance that they are dealing with a firm with their interests central to the corporate culture.	▪ Products that take advantage of customers' lack of understanding can backfire as customers either ask more insightful questions (with growing consumer awareness) or find that the services and products fall short of reasonable expectations.

(*Continued*)

TABLE 5.2 (*Continued*)

Example Issue	Ethical Outcomes	Compliant Outcomes
After-sales service	■ Prompt and efficient administration with low error rates and giving clear, understandable information and updates keeps consumer confidence and ongoing engagement (with possible future business). No unreasonable barriers to switching or changes.	■ Minimum information and administration leaves customers distant and uncertain. High barriers/charges/administration can cause customers to be trapped into holding an inappropriate product or service. Less likely to reengage and may cancel products early or unnecessarily.
Competence	■ Going beyond FCA Training and Competence. Taking higher level exams than required. Using CPD constructively and imaginatively. Getting engaged with the professional body. Offering a balanced, holistic, independent service putting the customer's needs first offers the level of professionalism that many consumers need and reasonably expect for important life-changing purchases. Clearly differentiated from sales and basic generic advice. Advisors clear about their scope, and refer on when not competent to advise on specialist areas.	■ Fulfilling only basic FCA T&C requirements. CPD just to fulfil in-firm hours requirements or keep regulators happy. Basic qualifications in a narrow field. ■ Stretching advice scope when pressed, rather than referring. ■ Customers do not feel they are receiving an open, professional, and independent service. May encourage some potential customers not to proceed with financial planning or to become cynical about commission-driven sales and therefore disengage.

Source: D. Jackman, *The Ethical Space.*

CONCLUSION

Culture is a useful construct for considering how ethics are translated into practice and how behaviours drive conduct risk—the new regulatory term for this area. We shall see in Chapter 10 the way in which structures within culture promulgate and create pro-compliance activity. It is these structures that are crucial for enabling and maintaining change in a positive direction.

Culture is one of the elements directed and controlled by governance; therefore we must consider more carefully how governance can become *good governance* in the next chapter.

ENDNOTES

1. Standard Chartered, *Group Code of Conduct,* p. 5, https://www.sc.com/en/resources/global-en/pdf/sustainabilty/Code_of_Conduct.pdf.
2. D. Walker et al., *A Review of Corporate Governance in UK Banks and Other Financial Industry Entities* (London: HM Treasury, 2009), http://webarchive.nationalarchives.gov.uk/+/http:/www.hm-treasury.gov.uk/d/walker_review_261109.pdf.
3. Financial Services Authority, *The Failure of the Royal Bank of Scotland: Financial Services Authority Board Report* (London: FSA, 2011), http://www.fsa.gov.uk/pubs/other/rbs.pdf.
4. Parliamentary Commission on Banking Standards, S2.19, *"An Accident Waiting to Happen": The Failure of HBOS* (London: House of Commons Stationery Office, 2013).
5. A. Saltz, *Saltz Review: An Independent Review of Barclays' Business Practices* (London: Barclays PLC, 2013), 76.
6. D. Jackman, *Training and Competence Sourcebook CP34* (London: FSA, 1999).
7. FSA, "TC2.1," *FCA Handbook* (London: FSA, 2013).
8. Bank of England Prudential Regulation Authority, *Prudential Regulation Authority Handbook* (London: Bank of England, 2013).
9. Ibid., TC 1.1.4.
10. D. Jackman, *An Ethical Framework for Financial Services* (2002), http://www.fsa.gov.uk/pubs/discussion/dp18.pdf.
11. Monetary Authority of Singapore, *Financial Advisers Act (CAP. 110) Guidelines on Fair Dealing—Board and Senior Management Responsibilities for Delivering Fair Dealing Outcomes to Customers* (Singapore: MAS, 2009).

12. Speech by Clive Adamson, Director of Supervision, the FCA, at the CFA Society–UK Professionalism Conference (London, April 19, 2013), http://www.fca.org.uk/news/regulation-professionalism.
13. FSA, *Treating Customers Fairly: Culture* (London: FSA, 2007), 4.
14. Ibid., idem.
15. Ibid., p. 16.
16. http://www.fsa.gov.uk/library/communication/pr/2012/087.shtml.

CHAPTER 6

Good Governance

And the reality:
The living men that I hate,
The dead man that I loved,
The craven man in his seat,
The insolent unreproved—
And no knave brought to book
Who has won a drunken cheer—
The witty man and his joke
Aimed at the commonest ear,
The clever man who cries
The catch cries of the clown,
The beating down of the wise
And great Art beaten down.

—W. B. Yeats, *The Fisherman* (1916)

Governance is the framework of systems and controls that shapes and determines ethics and culture and ensures the delivery of the businesses' aims and strategy. With the board at its head, and including possibly many levels of management, it is a framework engaged in providing direction and leadership, assurance, strategy, measurement, and monitoring control procedures. Some of the components have an important function as *checks-and-balances* functions, such as the standing board committees. External reporting, where appropriate, is usually coordinated by the company secretarial department and is concerned with accountability and transparency for shareholders, investors, customers, and other stakeholders. Taken as a whole, governance forms a complex outward-looking and inward-facing structure. For the sake of brevity, our focus here will be on those aspects that relate to compliance and regulators.

WHY DOES GOVERNANCE MATTER?

Corporate governance is central to the effective and efficient running of any organisation or business. It directs and shapes everything that comprises a business, from setting the long-term direction of the company to monitoring at least the outlines of its everyday operation, and thereby plays an important part in the organisation's ongoing success or failure.

So governance is a subject of importance to compliance, which needs to ensure suitable culture, standards, and customer outcomes are delivered, and to regulators who are concerned with the effective and consistent delivery of regulatory objectives. Both see governance as a part of the systems and control function of internal management. Consumers or business partners might well develop an interest in a company's governance arrangements in the course of deciding whether to undertake business with the company or purchase its services. Similarly, a potential buyer may well undertake due diligence that includes a focus on governance as an indicator of resilience and future prospects. Indeed, investors of all kinds may use measures of governance as a proxy for evaluating the wider health and sustainability of a potential investment.

Since 2008 regulators, particularly in financial services, have come to seize on governance as a legitimate focus of interest and evaluation since failures in governance are seen as significant contributing factors to the collapse of firms and banks. Governance has been seized upon as the key driver in delivering regulatory outcomes and a litmus test of compliance culture. That is not to say that individual responsibilities of board members did not matter before 2008, but the ability of regulators to effectively measure board performance and to take action where necessary was lacking.

The renewed focus on governance comes as a further extension of stage 4 of the General Model, where regulators are adding a focus on causes and prevention. Governance is thus reinforcing the shift in approach that includes other causal factors such as ethics and culture. This is the distinctive feature of stage 4, whereas stage 5 is marked out by a focus on outcomes and understanding the role of institutions in the community.

Governance will have been of interest to regulators for some time before reaching stage 4 but it has been difficult to approach in a systematic way. In the UK the scandals that led to the Cadbury Review in the early 1990s alerted regulators to the importance of board composition and behaviour and the need for quality non-executive directors to join boards. Rulebooks have "fitness and properness" tests as part of the individual registration process and authorisation requirements for new directors, and these form part of the *threshold conditions* for firm licensing. However, the tests are often perfunctory and rely on self-declaration. The only central checks for many regulators are still simple checks of outstanding court judgments and records of outstanding fines or debts. It is a negative screening only, and the numbers of applicants prevented from taking up their intended role is slight. The one advantage is to make credible any banning of individuals as part of a previous enforcement action, or a disqualification of directors under the companies acts, by preventing such people from re-entering the sector. The training and competence rules of many regulators do not bite on senior directors, although there has been some emphasis on directors keeping up to date through relevant CPD (continuing professional development) programmes and recently further discussion of the desirability of qualifications such as the UK Institute of Directors' chartered director programme.

Since 2008 governance has been seen as the basis for providing a holistic view of the health and compliance of a company as much as a set of specific requirements applying to boards and directors. Governance is, therefore, a route for focusing on systems and controls in general, and effective mechanisms of collective and individual accountability and reporting rather than to an antiseptic or insurance policy against wrongdoing or sloppy practices throughout the organisation.

Some recent cases show poor standards of governance to be at the heart of the regulatory and compliance problem. FSA/FCA's detailed report on the failure of RBS[1] cites considerable governance shortcomings and wider concerns have emerged from rate rigging, money laundering cases, and more generally "rewards for failure."[2] High-profile, celebrity cases such as the investigations into phone hacking by *The News of the World* and others in the UK have increased public interest in governance. Shareholder activism is also on the rise (partly as a result of the FRC (Financial Reporting Council) Stewardship Code), forcing in some unsuccessful directors and CEOs to step down.[3] Governance is now a headline subject and corporate governance is everyone's business.

Regulators of all kinds place great emphasis on the need for boards to consider the spirit of the rules rather than just the letter. Intent is key. Many of the reports picking over the failings of 2008[4] conclude that it is the behavioural drivers that are more significant in success or disaster than organisational or process points. Consequently, the culture and behaviour of the board are relevant and the provisions in the previous chapter apply equally to the board.

WHAT IS CORPORATE GOVERNANCE?

Our starting point is in the United Kingdom, as the Cadbury Report of 1992 is the first clear report and statement of modern-day corporate governance issues and standards anywhere. The Cadbury findings and recommendations form the basis of most international and national codes. The Cadbury Code that followed from the Report was a response, as many codes are, to a series of scandals, including the collapse of Poly Peck and BCCI and the appropriation of pension funds by Maxwell newspapers.

Cadbury defined corporate governance as:

- "The system by which companies are directed and controlled"[5]

The key elements are:

- "Boards of directors are responsible for the governance of their companies."
- Shareholders appoint the directors and the auditors and satisfy themselves that an appropriate governance structure is in place.

The key roles and responsibilities are:

- Setting the company's strategic aims, providing the leadership to put them into effect, supervising the management of the business, and reporting to shareholders on their stewardship

Cadbury also defined some basic ethics of governance as:

- Openness
- Integrity
- Accountability

The Cadbury report was followed in the UK by:

- 1995 Greenbury Report, which focussed on directors' remuneration
- 1998 Hampel Report, which combined these codes into the 'Combined Code'
- 1999 Turnbull Report, focussing on obligations for internal controls
- 2003 Higgs Report on the role of non-executive directors

These codes were all incorporated into the UK Combined Code, which became in June 2010 'The UK Corporate Governance Code.' In all of these the Cadbury definition is carried forward and expanded.

The Board's Role

The role of the board is central to these early reports although they also set out the roles of others. The board's role is developed in Higgs[6] as:

> The board is collectively responsible for promoting the success of the company by directing and supervising the company's affairs. The board's role is to provide entrepreneurial leadership of the company within a

framework of prudent and effective controls which enable risk to be assessed and managed. The board should set the company's strategic aims, ensure that the necessary financial and human resources are in place for the company to meet its objectives, and review management performance. The board should set the company's values and standards and ensure that its obligations to its shareholders and others are understood and met.

The core functions of governance are:

- Entrepreneurial leadership
- Risk management
- Long-term strategy
- Performance review
- Setting values, culture, and standards

These key elements remain as irreducible pillars of governance activity and responsibility internationally.

Governance in Singapore

The new Singapore Corporate Governance Code,[7] for example, follows the Higgs wording and adds, interestingly, new ideas in parts (d) and (f).

> **The Singapore Corporate Governance Code (May 2012)**
> The Board's role is to:
>
> (a) Provide entrepreneurial leadership, set strategic objectives, and ensure that the necessary financial and human resources are in place for the company to meet its objectives;
> (b) Establish a framework of prudent and effective controls which enables risks to be assessed and managed, including safeguarding of shareholders' interests and the company's assets;
> (c) Review management performance;
> (d) Identify the key stakeholder groups and recognise that their perceptions affect the company's reputation;
> (e) Set the company's values and standards (including ethical standards), and ensure that obligations to shareholders and other stakeholders are understood and met; and
> (f) Consider sustainability issues, e.g., environmental and social factors, as part of its strategic formulation.[8]

Bank of International Settlements

The Bank of International Settlements (BIS) sets out more detailed principles for an overall framework for interlocking controls for banks and this can apply to any organization.

Management Oversight and the Control Culture:

Principle 1: The board of directors should have responsibility for approving and periodically reviewing the overall business strategies and significant policies of the bank; understanding the major risks run by the bank, setting acceptable levels for these risks and ensuring that senior management takes the steps necessary to identify, measure, monitor and control these risks; approving the organisational structure; and ensuring that senior management is monitoring the effectiveness of the internal control system. The board of directors is ultimately responsible for ensuring that an adequate and effective system of internal controls is established and maintained.

Principle 2: Senior management should have responsibility for implementing strategies and policies approved by the board; developing processes that identify, measure, monitor and control risks incurred by the bank; maintaining an organisational structure that clearly assigns responsibility, authority and reporting relationships; ensuring that delegated responsibilities are effectively carried out; setting appropriate internal control policies; and monitoring the adequacy and effectiveness of the internal control system.

Principle 3: The board of directors and senior management are responsible for promoting high ethical and integrity standards, and for establishing a culture within the organisation that emphasises and demonstrates to all levels of personnel the importance of internal controls. All personnel at a banking organisation need to understand their role in the internal controls process and be fully engaged in the process.

Comply or Explain

The *comply or explain* approach is the trademark of corporate governance in the UK and many other countries that follow a similar style. It has been in operation since the UK Code's beginnings and is the foundation of the Code's flexibility. It is strongly supported by both companies and shareholders and allows a company to explain circumstances where good governance can be achieved by other means than by complying directly with the Governance Code. Chairpersons' statements must show why the course of action taken is preferable and this is open to challenge by shareholders. Unnecessarily, the FRC is particularly concerned about bland statements that add nothing to understanding. The FRC says:

> Above all, the personal reporting on governance by chairmen as the leaders of boards might be a turning point in attacking the fungus of "boiler-plate" which is so often the preferred and easy option in sensitive areas but which is *dead communication*.[9]

A great deal of effort and cost can be expended on corporate reporting, some millions of pounds per year for large organisations, but superficial comments, bland language, and apparent obfuscation can be counterproductive. However, the principle is that:

> Satisfactory engagement between company boards and investors is crucial to the health of the corporate governance regime. Companies and shareholders both have responsibility for ensuring that "comply or explain" remains an effective alternative to a rules-based system. There are practical and administrative obstacles to improved interaction between boards and shareholders. But certainly there is also scope for an increase in trust which could generate a virtuous upward spiral in attitudes to the Code and in its constructive use.[10]

Compliance is part of governance and we need to set compliance appropriately so it can both play its correct part and use the governance structures and mechanisms to achieve compliance and regulatory aims. To do these, we have developed the concept of *good governance*, drawing together the ethical and cultural considerations in the previous two chapters. Taken together these form a coherent section of regulatory and compliance development that forms stage 4 of the general model in Chapter 2—focusing, as we have seen, on causes of failure and prevention.

A MODEL OF GOOD GOVERNANCE

Good governance combines effectiveness and ethics. It assumes compliance with statutory regulations.

The Cadbury Code and earlier versions of the Combined Code formulated governance in terms of "having systems and controls in place," the implied basis being that "good process delivers good results." But managing via systems and controls is, in some senses, managing around the edge: setting boundaries, taking the temperature remotely, and considering key performance indicators and exception reporting, often through crude red-amber-green dashboards. Focus on the remote monitoring of process creates a vacuum, a hole in the centre, and prioritises the form of governance over its substance.

Processes are necessarily detached, dehumanised, and mechanical. They avoid ethics, culture, and any sense of values. Boards are not meant to get their 'hands dirty'; in fact there needs to be a proper separation between executive responsibility and non-executive oversight. But boards can also be easily drawn into a kind of displacement activity that provides comfort without accountability and beguiling improvements without real pain. This is a process that allows companies to dodge issues if they want to, to hide behind comply-and-explain clauses in governance codes and escape making difficult decisions. It is an opportunity to address symptoms rather than causes, inputs rather than end results.

This is a dangerous detachment that allows discontinuities to develop between a rarefied world of the board view and the realities of customer experience and engine room. Boards may well rely on regulators to do the joined-up, broader ethical thinking for them while resenting their supposed intrusion. This outsourcing of good governance can be seen to be creating a systemic culture of dependency that is proving very hard to break.

The values-free systems-and-control approach leads to a detachment from outcome (see Chapter 7) that in turn legitimises a penchant for quick fixes and superficial data. A faith in sound process allowed many boards to miss the obvious for the sake of fine detail in 2008. To many outsiders looking on or experiencing the side-effects, this appears as an absence of common sense. Companies need to look inside more purposively, maybe by discarding reliance on familiar tools, assumptions, and comfort blankets along the way.

So we can consider good governance under three headings:

1. *Compliance* with relevant codes, regulations, and best practises
2. *Effectiveness:* The capacity of internal governance systems and controls
3. *Ethics:* Commitment to a values-led culture (see Chapter 5) and external engagement (see Chapter 8)

The first is largely about meeting externally set expectations often set at a minimum level for the operation of effective markets and for shareholder and consumer protection. The second and third point more towards the internally set values and standards of an organisation—its systems and controls, fitness and properness, and wider role and purpose. In particular, it is important to identify the levels to which it aspires and how these match with everyday reality.

TEN PRINCIPLES OF GOOD GOVERNANCE

Here are 10 key themes that contribute to transforming everyday governance into a more effective and ethical system that we might call "good governance." These 10 themes should be considered as a whole and do not form an exclusive list.

Principle 1: Leadership

The board's primary role is to provide leadership for the organisation that enables it to meet its aims and fulfil its responsibilities. This leadership should be clear and run through all layers of the organisation, supported and given structure by clear lines of responsibility, reporting, and accountability. Leadership entails assessing and taking risks so that the company can grow and be entrepreneurial, as well as being prudent, controlling risk, and minimising shocks or damage to the system. It also includes a company choosing to take a lead in its sector or a group of companies taking initiatives for their general advancement or other, for example, national, interests.

Leadership encompasses setting direction, with goals and milestones, and the values and standards of the company by which it intends to operate and be known. This ethical piece is often neglected or simplified in a mission statement rather than being applied in practise, which may involve some real cost.

Leadership is individual and collective. The chairperson leads the board, collectively the board leads the company, and management translate that, demonstrably, into operation. Tone at the top needs to be supportive, or other initiatives to build ethical culture become difficult and potentially undermined. Staff cynicism and lack of confidence is quickly established if they observe senior managers and directors saying one thing and then doing something different in practice or finding shortcuts when the pressure mounts.

There is so much existing literature on the importance of leadership that it is not intended to add to that here, but by emphasising other dimensions of good governance the implication is that leadership, while important, is not the only factor and may have received a little too much attention, relatively speaking. There may be a limited amount that, once constituted, a board or any outsiders can do to much improve this dimension. The more effective lever is perhaps the constitution of the board in the first place and how it is strengthened and evolved (see Principle 3).

Principle 2: Independence

Nobody and no decision should be influenced inappropriately and no one person or group or interest should influence the company disproportionately. This points to a degree of healthy challenge and honed or balanced judgments, not autocratic direction. It is more likely that decisions made in the round will be of better quality and will have greater buy-in and longevity than those made by a few or in a doctrinal way. For this to happen successfully a number of hygiene factors need to be present. On these assumptions much of corporate governance is based.

The first of those factors is that those making decisions are independent of inappropriate influence. This needs to be actual and demonstrable, should any question be brought to bear at any time. There is a structural and an individual element to this.

What Does Independence Mean? For individuals, independence comes from strength of character and knowing one's mind, but in this context this is seen to be possible when the following conditions or qualities occur:

- *Competence:* Business and regulatory.
- *Negotiation, presentation, persuasion, leadership, facilitation, listening and communication skills:* Especially the chairperson.
- *Financial freedom:* Non-executive directors are not dependent on the financial return from a decision or action. This may mean for non-executive directors (NEDs) that they receive a relatively low remuneration so that they can exercise their judgment uninfluenced by any possible return from the outcome. A fee of £1,000 per day is emerging as a widely used reasonable benchmark for NED involvement. Difficulties arise when directors' pay is based on performance or is on a commission basis. This is explored further ahead.
- *Career freedom:* Independence is difficult if participants in any process are mindful of their next promotion or reputation. At least executives need to have an understanding that they can express opinions openly without fear of disadvantage or retribution. NEDs have a useful position here in that they have usually had successful careers and are not dependent upon preferment. They are also not part of the company career structure. They ought to be concerned about public reputation, but not unduly, although in some circumstances this may be something that spurs them on to make unpopular stands, if it seems to them to be necessary.

Specific attempts to breach independence such as voting irregularities, hiding or using misleading information, corruption, or inducements are usually all serious offences in general law.

Independence is also protected and promoted by other structural safeguards, specifically:

- Division of responsibility between significant roles (under the UK Corporate Governance Code this is a separation of chair and chief executive responsibilities, but in Germany, for example, the division may be between supervisory and executive boards).
- A majority or significant proportion of the board being non-executives.
- Democratic and open nomination, selection, and election of board directors.
- Regular reelection of directors and chairpersons (annual in the UK).

- Resignation statements of NEDs being made to the chair (there may be other arrangements for whistleblowers; the *Sunday Times* voted the whistleblowing CEO of Olympus as Businessman of the Year, 2011[11]).
- Time-limits on holding directorships for NEDs (considered to be 6 to 9 years in UK, after which they may be considered captured by the interests of the board or other directors).
- Transparency of records (for example, who made what decision when, and when did they know something) leading to individual and collective accountability.
- Senior independent director as a go-between between shareholders and the board and a sounding board for the chair.

Connected Parties Some codes seek to define non-independent relationships so as to be clear about what might be considered an independent director or advisor. This is particularly important in family-run companies. For example, the Singapore Governance Code sets out a series of relationships that cannot be described as independent:

> An "independent" director is one who has no relationship with the company, its related corporations, its substantial shareholders or its officers that could interfere, or be reasonably perceived to interfere, with the exercise of the director's independent business judgement with a view to the best interests of the company. The Board should identify in the company's annual report each director it considers to be independent. The Board should determine, taking into account the views of the Nominating Committee, whether the director is independent in character and judgement and whether there are relationships or circumstances which are likely to affect, or could appear to affect, the director's judgement. Directors should disclose to the Board any such relationship as and when it arises. The Board should state its reasons if it determines that a director is independent notwithstanding the existence of relationships or circumstances which may appear relevant to its determination, including the following:
>
> (a) a director being employed by the company or any of its related corporations for the current or any of the past three financial years;
> (b) a director who has an immediate family member who is, or has been in any of the past three financial years, employed by the company or any of its related corporations and whose remuneration is determined by the remuneration committee;
> (c) a director, or an immediate family member, accepting any significant compensation from the company or any of its related corporations for

the provision of services, for the current or immediate past financial year, other than compensation for board service;

(d) a director,
   (i) who, in the current or immediate past financial year, is or was; or
   (ii) whose immediate family member, in the current or immediate past financial year, is or was, a substantial shareholder of, or a partner in (with 5% or more stake), or an executive officer of, or a director of, any organisation to which the company or any of its subsidiaries made, or from which the company or any of its subsidiaries received, significant payments or material services (which may include auditing, banking, consulting and legal services), in the current or immediate past financial year. As a guide, payments aggregated over any financial year in excess of S$200,000 should generally be deemed significant;

(e) a director who is a substantial shareholder or an immediate family member of a substantial shareholder of the company; or

(f) a director who is or has been directly associated with a substantial shareholder of the company, in the current or any of the past three financial years.

Note:

The term "substantial shareholder" shall have the same meaning as currently defined in the Companies Act (Chapter 50 of the statutes of Singapore) (the "Companies Act"), i.e., a person who has an interest or interests in one or more voting shares in the company and the total votes attached to that share, or those shares, is not less than 5% of the total votes attached to all the voting shares in the company. "Voting shares" exclude treasury shares.

The term "immediate family" shall have the same meaning as currently defined in the Listing Manual of the Singapore Exchange (the "Listing Manual"), i.e., the person's spouse, child, adopted child, step-child, brother, sister and parent.

CASE STUDY: Ireland

A survey carried out by a professional services firm in Dublin (Resources Global Professionals working with the author), showed that maybe the importance of independence has not been learned by large corporations in Ireland. Using the scoring system, based solely on publically available information, 39 percent of Irish listed companies appear to be falling below the accepted governance standards for independence compared to their counterparts listed in the FTSE 100 in London.

The data collated and analysed in conjunction with University College Dublin (UCD) shows that in a series of straightforward comparisons between ISEQ and FTSE 100 listed companies—in the key sectors of food production, aviation, financial services, and construction—Irish companies come up short.

The Irish Corporate Governance Code, which directly reflects the UK version (based on the Combined Code first devised by Sir Adrian Cadbury in 1992), requires a raft of restraints within the corporate board and committee structures to try to allow non-executive directors to be as effective as possible and to protect their role. For example, the Code requires that over half the board are independent non-executives so that they can hold the balance of power in a tight, potentially crucial decision affecting outside stakeholders. Also the principles lead towards the chair and CEO being unable to dominate the crucial committees that set pay (the Remuneration Committee) and select new board members (the Nomination Committee). The intention is to restrain the influence chairpersons and senior executives have in determining their own pay and bonuses and recruiting their "lookalikes," friends, family, or associates to the board.

The most significant differences between Irish ISEQ firms and similar sections of the FTSE 100 were:

- 57 percent of ISEQ companies (16/28) failed to meet the independence standards for Nomination Committees in the ISEQ Combined Code, compared to 1 in the FTSE 100 comparative sample.
- 32 percent (9/28) of ISEQ companies failed to meet similar standards in relation to the Remuneration Committees, whereas none failed this test in the comparable FTSE companies.
- 46 percent of ISEQ companies (13/28) failed to have Remuneration Committees of sufficient size, allowing them to be dominated by the COE or chair, compared to 2 in the FTSE.
- 32 percent (9/28) of ISEQ companies had senior independent non-executive directors of over 9 years' standing (considered to be too long and to compromise their independence), or were not clearly independent, compared to none in FTSE.
- Most significantly, 29 percent (8/28) of ISEQ companies did not have the required 50 percent of independent directors. Therefore, independents could not form a majority and resist executive action. No companies in the FTSE fall below the 50 percent mark.

These reflect wider cultural assumptions, but because they all point in the same direction, we can say that Irish corporations seem to place less value on independence at board level than their UK counterparts. The conclusion focuses on the maturity of the corporate community and its ability and willingness to accept diverse viewpoints, challenge and test assumptions and strategies, and look outwards for inspiration and counterbalance.

Principle 3: Composition and Diversity

The board needs the necessary balance of expertise and up-to-date experience to contribute effectively to any debate or action. This may include technical expertise and knowledge of the business and regulations. It may be necessary for an individual to ask for extra specific information and advice and the company should be prepared to source and fund that advice up to a reasonable level.

The board may choose to determine that some directors, such as lawyers, compliance experts, and accountants—who are appointed for their specific knowledge—may need to hold relevant qualifications and hold up-to-date practising certificates, and carry out CPD where necessary. This may limit the pool of those suitable for these roles. One of these executives, or an additional executive, should have specific responsibility for regulatory compliance, where necessary.

The core competences for all boards could include some or all of the following:

- Vision and understanding of the ethics, roles, and values of the sector and their practical application
- Leadership of people and community business; the ability to hold management to account and to challenge information and recommendations
- Business knowledge of the products and services offered and the issues faced
- Regulatory and legal understanding up to a level that allows the board to fulfil its duties
- Analysis—the ability to discern the financial position of the business from the information available, the completeness, accuracy, and veracity of that information, the ability to identify risks and opportunities, and the ability to ensure that proper reporting and evaluation are undertaken

The appropriate balance of skills, experience, and competences necessary across the board as a whole would be:

- Specific business experience of over 10 years in relevant functions
- Accountancy and audit experience of over 10 years
- Legal experience
- Regulatory experience
- Community engagement and consumer protection experience in relevant sectors
- Company secretarial experience

External Evaluation It is increasingly considered helpful to have an external evaluation of the board's competence and composition, as well as its effectiveness, on a regular basis, or at least every three years. If it is used, it allows observations to be depersonalised and for the evaluation to have more credibility outside the organization. It is also useful to have a second opinion on board competence and processes. This may be sought independently of the advice from auditors.

TABLE 6.1 Levels of board competence.

Competence	Threshold	Developmental	Secure	Leadership
Personal/ interpersonal	Confidence in own board contribution	Learning new areas; builds communication skills	Manages complexity	Consensus building; winning buy-in
Governance/ decision making	Applies regulatory standards Reliable and frequent input	Makes specific input bringing step change	Critical thinking Constructive challenge	Valued judgment Decisive
Technical/ business	Overall awareness of sector	Technical insight into products	System design and solution finding	Sophisticated input to business processes
Strategic vision/ learning	Understands company value	Scanning horizon	Evaluating business plans	Participates in sectoral agenda setting
Regulatory/ risk/legal	Basic requirements	Risk-based systems focus	Thorough audit Mitigation	Long-term plan and regulatory relationship
Integrity/ethics	Fulfils fit-and-proper (F&P) basic standards	Commitment to wider corporate purpose	Stakeholder engagement	Acts on outcomes and stakeholder responsibilities

Diversity   We have established that for independence to be meaningful, directors need the necessary competence and confidence to challenge and that an open culture is necessary. If a range of views and questions is useful, it is vital to have contributors and participants who come from a range of standpoints and experiences. This is what diversity means, although it is often focused on the level of female gender representation on boards and in certain, often public roles, and also on ethnic representation.

The Sir David Walker Review of 2009 is clear about the value of women on boards but also recognises the challenges:

> Despite the importance of improving diversity ... it would be unrealistic to expect to reduce the present unfortunate gender imbalance by "parachuting" into boardrooms as NEDs women without executive board or senior executive experience elsewhere. The first focus of initiative should thus be in promoting the development of women to take senior executive and executive board positions within companies in which they are employed. This will be an essential element in boosting the scale and diversity of the pool of talent available to fill NED positions ... elsewhere.[12]

Research carried out by the author showed that in 2009, only 10.6 percent of FTSE main board directors were women.[13] In February 2011, Lord Davis published his review into this issue and recommended that UK listed companies in the FTSE 100 should aim for a minimum of 25 percent female board member representation by 2015. This has not been achieved.

The Walker Review also highlighted the need to allow younger people to gain experience so that they could come to main boards better equipped. In conclusion, Walker says that the point is to avoid executive or board *groupthink*. The EU has proposed (October 2012) quotas for female representation on boards, though there is resistance to this (for example, the "30% club" wanting women to succeed through their own efforts).

Competence   Building competence of the board is assisted by:

- Directors' induction programme and regular updating (continuous professional development—CPD) on such areas as compliance from the in-house compliance team and/or from independent advisors.
- Freedom to receive information that is accurate, timely, and complete.
- Freedom to obtain additional information, advice, or support from any part of the company or outside from specialists—funded by the company.
- Regular (annual) appraisal or evaluation of the board and the chair, some elements being public or available for inspection. For FTSE 350 this evaluation should be externally facilitated every three years (the facilitator's connection with the company should be made clear).

The amount of time available for NEDs has also been an issue that has attracted attention. In the UK 36 days per year is a recommended allotment of time for NEDs so that they can appreciate the issues concerned but not become captured by their financial relationships with the company concerned. Attendance of directors at meetings is essential and the number of meetings as coupled with levels of attendance can be a measure of board and committee effectiveness.

In addition, many firms must satisfy regulators that individual directors pass a fit-and-proper test. This includes requirements in:

- Honesty, integrity, and reputation
- Competence and capability

Detailed requirements may apply and registration is often required.

Principle 4: Constructive Challenge

This is an extension of the constructive challenge element of crucibles designed to foster values-led culture (see Chapters 4 and 5) applied here to the board specifically and connected governance structures such as committees.

Central to the effectiveness of independence is the ability of the board of the company, especially non-executives, to offer constructive and effective challenge. This is partly a function of individuals' competence and confidence, but also the climate set by the chair in accepting and fostering open and honest debate. This may be on a Chatham House basis (i.e., not recorded) so that there are fewer worries about "who said what." Ultimately, key differences need to be minuted so that any honest differences of opinion can be clear later, but the company can show that these differences were aired and a conclusion reached through a process of debate and resolution. It is the basis of tough judgments that are so often important later and the way in which differences are resolved.

Independence of compliance (and non-executive directors) is important to achieve higher quality, ethical decision making and to challenge the assumptions and lazy habits that creep into corporate culture.

As we saw in Chapters 4 and 5, challenge processes are frameworks that both allow challenge to occur and provide a structure for questioning that is flexible but also enabling and organised. They give board members permission for questions to be raised that might not otherwise be brought forward without fear of embarrassment.

Constructive challenge processes are frameworks that are depersonalised and allow for questions to be raised, for example:

- Determining strategy
- Product design
- Compliance monitoring

- Sales processes
- Face-to-face advice
- Management meetings

Decisions don't happen in a vacuum; they reflect the environment from which they come. It is the responsibility of governance structures to shape and *consciously* create a framework in which it is more likely that positive and compliant behaviour will occur on a consistent basis.

This corporate culture is an embedded environment that is set by a carefully constructed combination of carrots, sticks, and inspirations. It includes new strategies, targets, limits and trigger points, policy reformulations, tone-at-the-top, communications, reporting requirements, leadership, and compliance interventions that will take the organisation in the right direction.

The creation of a coherent and resilient culture is founded on clear, collective values, standards, ethics, and a sense of purpose—all of which must be set by the board. Indeed, the preface to the current Financial Reporting Council's (FRC) UK Corporate Governance Code 2012 requires boards *"to think deeply and spend time considering the spirit of the code and its principles rather than focusing on the letter or seeking to game the rules."*[14]

To reduce prescription and to give boards more scope requires careful and more skilful management than traditional control. It may require different directors or different skills. Certainly decisions and actions need boundaries and limits, and there must be the safety net of exception reporting. Yet the real advantages come from setting people in the right direction. This means clarity about purpose.

Principle 5: Quality of Decision Making and Judgments

Good governance requires a direct focus on judgment. It is not enough to go through good process and "show your work" if a board or company then goes on to make a flawed decision. Decisions at the board have to be shown (i.e., minuted) to be closely debated, analysed, stress-tested, and evaluated so that the opportunity for failure is diminished to near-zero. The test in this area is very high. Board evaluation by external parties or by regulators is here to stay.

So governance has a legitimate reason for a laser-like, forensic examination of how and why decisions are made at all levels. Companies need to demonstrate:

- How good decision making is supported and facilitated
- How the chairperson demonstrates effectiveness

- How the NEDs individually and collectively make a contribution
- How decisions are recorded and reported
- When and whom you call for external advice

Regulators' orthodoxy used to include an unwillingness to judge judgments. Now it is the norm and the core of recent enforcement actions. Governance needs to respond.

Questions to Ask Careful thought has to be given by NEDs as to the right questions to ask. The UK Governance Code (Combined Code) in its 2003 version includes some questions for new NEDs to ask:

- What is the company's current financial position and what has its financial track record been over the last three years?
- What are the key dependencies (e.g., regulatory approvals, key licences, etc.)?
- What record does the company have on corporate governance issues?
- If the company is not performing particularly well, is there potential to turn it around, and do I have the time, desire, and capability to make a positive impact?
- What is the company's attitude towards, and relationship with, its shareholders?
- Is there anything about the nature and extent of the company's business activities that would cause me concern both in terms of risk and any personal ethical considerations?
- Am I satisfied that the internal regulation of the company is sound and that I can operate effectively within its stated corporate governance framework?

It is clear in the 2010 UK Governance Code that the chair is responsible for creating the open culture that fosters debate and challenge and he or she needs to have the right qualities of facilitation and listening to allow this to happen.

The 2010 UK Governance code requires boards:

To follow the spirit of the Code to good effect, boards must think deeply, thoroughly and on a continuing basis, about their overall tasks and the implications of these for the roles of their individual members. Absolutely key in this endeavour are the leadership of the chairman of a board, the support given to and by the CEO, and the frankness and openness of mind with which issues are discussed and tackled by all directors.[15]

Constructive Challenge Frameworks Constructive challenge frameworks allow challenge to occur in a non-unusual, depersonalised, and measured way and provide a structure for questioning that is flexible but also enabling and organised. They give permission for questions to be raised that might not otherwise be brought forward without fear of embarrassment, detriment, or career awkwardness. And they are built up from principles and values that the firm has pre-decided are important and useful.

It is crucial that such ethics and principles are neither ideologically driven—we are not suggesting a moralistic ethiocracy—nor purely bottom line, as this is not a business case. The key is complexity. Crucibles bring together the long term and short, the individual and collective perspective, the outcomes and good process, the transcendent and the visceral.

Constructive challenge can follow a similar structure to that used in structured questions in resolving ethical issues. As many questions may be ethical in nature the crucible approach will often replace the ethical models used in earlier stages of development. Crucibles are a more developed tool. Here is one example of questions for the constructive challenge process, first set out in 2002 and now reflected in many regulators and firm systems. This example uses as a basis the core ethics and values delineated in Chapter 4 as the basis of regulatory and compliance objectives, but they are also perfectly sound business values:

Open, Honest, Responsive, and Accountable Groups:
- Who is left out or kept in the dark? Why?
- How happy are we to be associated with our decisions/actions?
- Are we listening or just hearing?
- What can we learn? How do we help others to understand us?
- How do we recognise and deal with conflicts of interest?

Relating to Colleagues and Customers Fairly and with Respect:
- Do we treat everyone as we would like to be treated?
- Do we deal with people with respect and without prejudice?
- How do we keep rights and obligations in balance and proportionate?
- When do we hold to our commitments and resist "fudging"?
- Who benefits and who loses out? Should they?

Committed to Acting Competently, Responsibly, and Reliably:
- Do we do what we say we will do?
- Under pressure, do we swap cooperation for coercion?
- Do we dither or delay? How is error treated?
- Do people trust us? If not, why not?
- Can we meet our commitments and plans?

Developing Vision and a Values-Led Approach:

- What needs changing? What prevents change?
- What is the long-term outcome? What is sustainable?
- Do we sufficiently recognise and act on our stakeholder responsibilities?
- How do we develop shared purpose, loyalty, and fulfilment?
- Do we apply ethical criteria simply to gain an advantage or because we believe we should?[16]

Principle 6: Checks and Balances

The firm needs to have:

- Basic systems and controls to support good governance
- Board committees to manage key aspects of its role

Basic systems include:

- Clear and appropriate apportionment of responsibilities among senior management, including recording reporting lines, job descriptions, role responsibilities, and appraisal mechanisms
- Decision-making procedures
- Internal control mechanisms designed to secure compliance with decisions and procedures at all levels of the firm
- Internal reporting and communication of information at all levels of the firm
- Risk management
- Ensuring that individuals with significant management responsibility have sufficient time and resources to enable them to fulfil their responsibilities
- Adequate training and briefing of senior staff and the board
- Succession, delegation, and outsourcing arrangements
- Conflicts of interest and breaches registers
- Public registers of directors' interests, gifts, and entertainment
- Whistleblowing arrangements
- Codes of conduct, including personal account dealing rules

Segregation of Duties Where it is made possible and appropriate by the nature, scale, and complexity of its business, a firm should segregate the duties of individuals and departments in such a way as to reduce opportunities for financial crime or contravention of requirements and standards under the regulatory system. For example, the duties of front-office and back-office staff should be segregated so as to prevent a single individual initiating, processing, and controlling transactions. The performance of multiple functions should not prevent those from discharging any particular functions soundly, honestly, and professionally.

Segregation of duties should be designed to:

1. Prevent conflicts of interest.
2. Ensure no one individual is completely free to commit assets or incur liabilities, that is, to:
   - Initiate a transaction.
   - Bind the firm.
   - Make payments.
   - Account for it.
3. Ensure the board receives objective and accurate information on financial performance, the risks faced, and the adequacy of systems.

Each should play a part in the decision-making process on all significant decisions. Both parties should demonstrate the qualities and application to influence strategy, day-to-day policy, and its implementation. This does not require their day-to-day involvement in the execution and implementation of policy. It does, however, require involvement in strategy and general direction, as well as knowledge of, and influence on, the way in which strategy is being implemented through day-to-day policy.

Board Committees The main checks on the board's operation in many jurisdictions are the four board committees. The UK Corporate Governance Code and especially in its 2003 version is very clear on how these should operate.[17] The nomination committee sets out the basics that apply to the rest.

Nomination Committee

The search for board candidates should be conducted, and appointments made, on merit, against objective criteria and with due regard for the benefits of diversity on the board, including gender. The board should satisfy itself that plans are in place for orderly succession for appointments to the board and to senior management, so as to maintain an appropriate balance of skills and experience within the company and on the board and to ensure progressive refreshing of the board.

B.2.1 There should be a nomination committee which should lead the process for board appointments and make recommendations to the board. A majority of the company of the nomination committee should be independent non-executive directors. The chairman or an independent non-executive director should chair the committee, but the chairman should not chair the nomination committee when it is dealing with the appointment of a successor to the chairmanship. The nomination committee should make available its terms of reference, explaining its role and the authority delegated to it by the board.

B.2.2 The nomination committee should evaluate the balance of skills, experience, independence, and knowledge on the board and, in the light of this evaluation, prepare a description of the role and capabilities required for a particular appointment.

B.2.3 Non-executive directors should be appointed for specified terms subject to re-election and to statutory provisions relating to the removal of a director. Any term beyond six years for a non-executive director should be subject to particularly rigorous review, and should take into account the need for progressive refreshing of the board.

B.2.4 A separate section of the annual report should describe the work of the nomination committee, including the process it has used in relation to board appointments. An explanation should be given if neither an external search consultancy nor open advertising has been used in the appointment of a chairman or a non-executive director.

On re-election it says:

All directors of FTSE 350 companies should be subject to annual election by shareholders. All other directors should be subject to election by shareholders at the first annual general meeting after their appointment, and to re-election thereafter at intervals of no more than three years.

Nonexecutive directors who have served longer than nine years should be subject to annual re-election. The names of directors submitted for election or re-election should be accompanied by sufficient biographical details and any other relevant information to enable shareholders to take an informed decision on their election.

The board should set out to shareholders in the papers accompanying a resolution to elect a non-executive director why they believe an individual should be elected. The chairman should confirm to shareholders when proposing re-election that, following formal performance evaluation, the individual's performance continues to be effective and to demonstrate commitment to the role.[18]

The remuneration, audit, and risk committees run on similar lines. The remuneration committee is considered in the next section.

Audit   Recent financial reporting reviews have redefined the role of the audit committee.[19] A few key points are:

1. The audit committee should review the significant financial reporting issues and judgements made in connection with the preparation of the

company's financial statements, interim reports, preliminary announcements and related formal statements.

2. It is management's, not the audit committee's, responsibility to prepare complete and accurate financial statements and disclosures in accordance with financial reporting standards and applicable rules and regulations. However the audit committee should consider significant accounting policies, any changes to them and any significant estimates and judgements.

3. The audit committee should review the company's internal financial controls (that is, the systems established to identify, assess, manage, and monitor financial risks); and unless expressly addressed by a separate board risk committee comprised of independent directors or by the board itself, the company's internal control and risk management systems.

4. The audit committee should monitor and review the effectiveness of the company's internal audit function. Where there is no internal audit function, the audit committee should consider annually whether there is a need for an internal audit function and make a recommendation to the board, and the reasons for the absence of such a function should be explained in the relevant section of the annual report.

External Audit Revisions to the system[20] include comments on selecting external auditors. This process is coming under increased scrutiny after the 2008 financial crisis.

1. The audit committee should have primary responsibility for making a recommendation on the appointment, reappointment, and removal of the external auditors. If the board does not accept the audit committee's recommendation, it should include in the annual report, and in any papers recommending appointment or reappointment, a statement from the audit committee explaining its recommendation and should set out reasons why the board has taken a different position.

2. The audit committee section of the annual report should explain to shareholders how it reached its recommendation to the board on the appointment, reappointment or removal of the external auditors. This explanation should normally include supporting information on tendering frequency, the tenure of the incumbent auditor, and any contractual obligations that acted to restrict the audit committee's choice of external auditors.

3. If the external auditor is being considered to undertake aspects of the internal audit function, the audit committee should consider the effect this may have on the effectiveness of the company's overall arrangements for internal control and investor perceptions in this regard.

Investor perceptions are likely to be influenced by:

- The rationale set out in the annual report for the work being performed by the external auditor
- The nature and extent of the work performed by the external auditor
- Whether, in the absence of internal audit work, the audit committee is wholly reliant on the views of the external auditor about the effectiveness of its system of controls relating to core activities and significant locations

Non-Audit Services The audit committee's objective should be to ensure that the provision of such services does not impair the external auditor's independence or objectivity. In this context, the audit committee should consider:

- Whether the skills and experience of the audit firm make it a suitable supplier of the non-audit services
- Whether there are safeguards in place to eliminate or reduce to an acceptable level any threat to objectivity and independence in the conduct of the audit resulting from the provision of such services by the external auditor
- The fees incurred, or to be incurred, for non-audit services both for individual services-related fee levels and the fee levels individually and in aggregate, relative to the audit fee
- The criteria that govern the compensation of the individuals performing the audit

As a consequence, careful consideration will be needed when determining whether it is in the interests of the company that the services should be purchased from the audit firm (rather than another supplier) and, if so, whether any safeguards to be put in place by the audit firm are likely to be effective, and how this will be disclosed in the annual report.

Principle 7: Whistleblowing

This is a very specific part of governance, allowing a safety valve for those who consider there may be impropriety occurring in the company and who feel unable to deal with this through their normal reporting channels. Often a whistleblowing helpline is offered—this may be to an external organisation that can mediate or to an NED in a small company.

The audit committee should review arrangements by which staff of the company may, in confidence, raise concerns about possible improprieties in matters of financial reporting or other matters. The audit committee's objective should be to ensure that arrangements are in place for the proportionate and independent investigation of such matters and for appropriate follow-up action.

What Is Whistleblowing? The official description for *whistleblowing* is "making a disclosure in the public interest," in other words, "blowing the whistle." It means that if you believe there is wrongdoing in your workplace (e.g., your employer is committing a criminal offence), you can report this by following the correct processes, and your employment rights are protected.

If someone decides to blow the whistle on an organisation, you are protected and your employer cannot victimise you (e.g., by not offering you a promotion or other opportunities your employer would have otherwise offered). Whistleblowers are protected for public interest, to encourage people to speak out if they find malpractice in an organisation or workplace.

EXAMPLE OF A WHISTLEBLOWING CODE

When should I speak up?

You must speak up when you see anyone:

- Breaking laws, including committing fraud or other criminal acts
- Breaking regulatory requirements
- Breaking codes of conduct, group, business, or country policies and procedures
- Not addressing control weaknesses
- Doing anything that may damage our reputation
- Hiding evidence of any of the above

You should speak up if you have a suspicion that any of these situations has taken place, is taking place, or is about to take place. You do not need to be certain of misconduct to report it. However, you must speak up in good faith. This means you must do so honestly and without malice.

You should not use this route to deal with general human-resource-related matters. Instead you should speak to your line manager or Human Resources, or should raise the issue under the Employee Grievance Procedures.

What do I do if I suspect misconduct?

There are a number of ways you can raise a concern if you see or suspect misconduct:

- Speak to your line manager.
- If you feel uncomfortable doing this, you should contact your Country Head of Compliance or a member of country senior management.
- If you feel you cannot raise your concerns with country senior management or Compliance, you should contact our independent service (People in Touch), who will pass your concern to Compliance anonymously if this is what you prefer.
- In exceptional circumstances, you can raise concerns directly with a relevant organization such as a regulator or external auditor. This would only be appropriate if the situation is extremely serious, or if in your view we had not dealt effectively with your disclosure.

Protected Disclosures For disclosure to be protected by the law, it should be made to the right person and in the right way:

- You must make the disclosure in good faith (which means with honest intent and without malice).
- You must reasonably believe that the information is substantially true.
- You must reasonably believe you are making the disclosure to the prescribed person.
- If you make a qualifying disclosure in good faith to your employer, or through a process that your employer has agreed, you are protected. You should check your employment contract to see if your employer has set out a process for whistleblowing.
- If you feel unable to make a disclosure to your employer, then there are other prescribed people you can make a disclosure to. If you are unsure, you should always get professional advice before going ahead. Anything you say to a legal advisor in order to get advice is automatically protected.
- You could make a qualifying disclosure to the person responsible for the area of concern to you. For example, you might raise concerns about health and safety with a health and safety representative.
- In some circumstances you may be able to make a disclosure to someone who isn't prescribed. More information on prescribed persons

is contained in the "Blowing the Whistle on Workplace Wrongdoing" article.[21]

Principle 8: Remuneration and Reward

Setting and monitoring remuneration is an important item of governance as it contributes to driving performance and setting the view and direction of the company. This operates at the front line in the way targets are set. The remuneration committee has a key role.

The committee should as a minimum:

1. Determine and agree with the board the framework or broad policy for the remuneration of the chief executive, the chair of the company, and such other members of the executive management as it is designated to consider.
2. Have delegated responsibility for setting remuneration for all executive directors, the chair, and, to maintain and assure their independence, the company secretary. The remuneration of non-executive directors shall be a matter for the chair and executive company of the board. No director or manager should be involved in any decisions as to their own remuneration.
3. Be exclusively responsible for establishing the selection criteria, selecting, appointing, and setting the terms of reference for any remuneration consultants who advise the committee.

Recent concern about pay levels, especially in financial services, and apparently high rates of reward even if there have not been sufficient improvements in performance, have led to in the UK:

- FCA Remuneration Code
- "Project Merlin"
- Bonus constraints by government
- FRC remuneration code

The FRC Governance code states:

Levels of remuneration should be sufficient to attract, retain and motivate directors of the quality required to run the company successfully, but a company should avoid paying more than is necessary for this purpose. A significant proportion of executive directors' remuneration should be structured so as to link rewards to corporate and individual performance.

- Deferred or staged bonuses are now considered so as to spread the impact and keep staff engaged.

- The balance between long-term (e.g., shares) and short-term rewards is key to developing long-term perspective.
- Clawbacks are possible where decisions or sales turn out to be unsuccessful.

Principle 9: Evaluation, Reporting, and Accountability

Evaluation principles apply to day-to-day or meeting-to-meeting monitoring of the company and annual appraisal and the lead-up to the external reporting cycle. All boards need to be evaluated, either by themselves or ideally by external parties annually, at least from time to time (externally every three years is the UK requirement). How this is conducted can help to lay the foundations for all other governance activities throughout the company. Evaluation depends on the criteria for assessment and this depends in turn on the overall purpose of the enterprise.

The Value of Independent External Advice There is an assumption that no one knows a business better than those who run it. That may be so; but a strong management can gain real additional value from receiving an external view and a range of differing perspectives. This value encompasses independent advice from within the board as non-executives *and* from external sources such as advisors and consultants. In this second category there is growing acknowledgment that true independence cannot come from audit firms who may be heavily invested in corporate positions and dependent on audit income. This public view is something that many companies urgently need to weigh and address.

At the core of governance is the concept of "independence." Independence delivers an objective view at the heart of the business and is, perhaps, the best insurance the company and the wider community have against corruption and calamity. Having an alternative voice can provide value through benchmarking best practice, identifying opportunities, broader vision, and access to contacts as well as technical expertise and improved risk management. Outsiders can see a company dispassionately, as a consumer, regulator, shareholder, or partner might do. Independence means not being constrained by an accepted line, an internal culture, or a vested interest.

But independence is a fragile and somewhat delicate corporate creature. Independence is easily undermined, compromised, restrained, and misrepresented. It may seem providential to present independence but it is of limited value if not secure and soundly based. Independence to be effective has to be high quality.

The Use of External Advice The UK Corporate Governance Code and the 2010 Walker Review (following the 2008 crisis) both recognised the need for independence as the acerbate and disinfectant of corporate governance. External advice has a special role in many circumstances, such as:

- Board members to have access to external advice (to improve understanding, clarification, or verification of executive recommendations)
- Board evaluation
- Audit of management information
- Risk management
- Compliance and regulatory expertise

In the 2012–2013 research carried out by the author on FTSE 100 companies it was found that:

- Only 35 percent companies conduct an external evaluation.
- Only 9 percent use an independent consultant.
- Only 56 percent use only internal evaluation.

This seems to be missing the opportunity that an external perspective can provide. To become unnecessarily introspective seems to be contrary to the outward-looking and open culture sought by most corporate governance codes including the UK and Irish Codes.

External input is not necessarily intrusive or expensive or unsettling. The skill is to be unobtrusive so the external evaluator can observe the dynamics and culture of the organisation. External advice needs to be sensitive to the values, ethics, and intent of the senior people and how these translate through the company. One of the common governance failures is a discontinuity between senior levels of direction and the "engine room" or frontline of the business that others encounter and that drives profitability.

External input can also be valuable in:

- Surveying the external environment and risk horizon
- Providing an independent view of governance practices
- Benchmarking against international standards
- Board training, updating, and mentoring
- NED induction

Regulatory Pressure The role of independence is not purely a matter of choice. The UK and Irish Governance codes require that directors, especially non-executive directors, have access to independent professional advice at the company's expense where they judge it necessary to discharge their responsibilities as directors. This is to ensure levels of competence but also to allow NEDs to obtain a wider and deeper perspective on a subject that is of great significance to the company. Through this open channel NEDs can provide higher standards of input and, critically for independence, they are not reliant only on the internal view of executives.

To reinforce this, new directors must receive a full, formal, and tailored induction on joining the board and it is essential that directors continually update their skills. The company is required by the Code to provide the necessary resources for developing and updating its directors' knowledge or capabilities and this is a major contribution that external advisors with a side international and sector-specific perspective can make.

FTSE and ISEQ listed companies, for example, are required to undertake annual board evaluations overseen by the chair. The chair is also subject to these standards, usually through a process run by the senior non-executive, but which is far better, given the close working relationships involved, carried out by a trusted independent party. To check progress and report transparently and credibly on board performance, the UK and Irish Codes, for example, require that an evaluation of the board should be externally facilitated at least every three years. The external facilitator should be as independent as possible, with a clear identification in the annual report of why they were chosen together with a statement as to whether they have any other connection with the company.

Scanning the Horizon A major contribution of an external advisor or independent evaluator is to be able to look outside and see the way the company is moving forward relative to the wider environment and peers. This includes scanning the horizon for new opportunities and identifying unexpected risks. This may be a process that seems too time-consuming within the normal business or can simply be too narrow, confirming preexisting models and assumptions. Outside advice can challenge assumptions.

Framework for Board Evaluation

Here is a checklist for your own or external board evaluation.

Board Structure

Number on board and responsibilities:

- Chair
- Vice chair
- Senior NED
- NEDs
- Executives

Staff reporting

Attendees

External specialists

Length of time served (i.e., over 9 years)

Representation

Committees:

- Nomination
- Risk and compliance
- Finance
- Audit

Frequency of meetings of each

Board Competences (Including Qualifications)

TABLE 6.2 Evaluating board competence.

Board Member	Business Experience	Accountancy or Financial	Legal or Regulatory	Community, Consumer, or Other

Roles and Responsibilities

- What is the precise role of the board and its committees?
- What is the scope and limitations of each?
- How do these interrelate?
- Are there any gaps or overlaps?
- How is the separation of responsibilities between non-executive and executive functions ensured?

- How are conflicts of interest identified, declared, reported, and managed?
- Does any policy or information or training exist?
- Whistleblowing arrangements
- Anti-bribery and anti-money-laundering obligations

Vision and Values

How does the board set out:

- The purpose of the company?
- The purpose of the board and committees?
- The vision for the company (short and long term)?
- Its values?
- The standards expected?
- Its stakeholders and community outcomes?

How are these discussed, expressed, communicated, evaluated, reported, and revised?

Board Behaviour

How does the board behave in terms of:

- Chair's leadership and facilitation of open and supportive culture?
- Constructive challenge?
- Contribution of new ideas/contacts/information?
- Mastery of information?
- Setting an example/tone?
- Consensual, timely, and effective decision making?
- Understanding responsibilities?
- Communication of decisions (including external reporting)?
  - Method of reporting internally
  - External reporting cycle
  - Special reporting (e.g., regulators)
- Financial probity?
- Follow-up of decisions, sanctions, and long-term development?

Risk and Compliance

- How does the board express the risk appetite of the company?
- How is risk reported to the board? Insert heat map, risk register, and dashboard?
- How is risk evaluated and reviewed?
- How does the company feed risk into its decision-making processes?
- How does the company identify and filter longer term risks (horizon scanning)?
- What is the compliance culture of the company?
- How is this being developed?
- What is the status, reporting line, exposure to the board, and resourcing of compliance and risk?
- How was a difficult issue handled?
- How does the company understand and evaluate consumer outcomes? (see Chapter 7)
- What is the relationship with the regulators?
- How is this being developed?

Strategy, Board Development, and Stakeholders

- What is the longer-term strategy?
- Do you have a specific board development plan?
  - CPD
  - Briefings and awareness sessions/updates
  - Succession planning
  - Long-term development
- What is the role, resourcing, and use of external advice and evaluation?
- How often is board evaluation carried out and by whom?
- What are the gaps self-identified? How are they being filled?
- Who are the company's stakeholders? How is materiality defined?
- What are the key impacts on stakeholders?
- How are the company and board engaging with stakeholders? How can this be improved?

- Does the company have a CSR policy? How is that valued?
- Does the company subscribe to any external accreditations?
- How does the company view sustainability and its contribution to community?

Information Flow

Follow a report into the board and the information flow out of it:

- How is it prepared?
- How is it presented and by whom?
- Challenges
- Minutes/other recording
- Decisions disseminated
- Wider communication
- Reporting
- Ongoing follow-up
- Re-submission

Financial Control

- How is credit risk evaluated and controlled?
- Is there sufficient capital reserve?
- How is liquidity ensured?
- What emergency wind-down or restoration arrangements exist?
- What is the longer-term view?
- What documentation is received by the board? How often?
- In what circumstances would the board be contacted between meetings?
- What are the business continuity plans?

Follow-Up

- What are the major strengths? What are the gaps? What is recommended?
- Immediate action?

Principle 10: External Engagement

Much has been made here of effective stakeholder engagement as a governance process. But beyond the Annual General Meeting (AGM), engagement can be stilted and artificial to the point of becoming superficial and devalued. It may be that it is not clear what the business case could be for communication beyond shareholders, Consequently, companies may be tempted to not devote sufficient resources with the result that they miss out on outcomes that are both imaginative and comprehensive.

Yet customers, potential customers, employees and potential employees, suppliers, policymakers, and regulators all have a significant role in maintaining a sustainable business. Businesses need to be mindful in an interconnected world of their legitimacy and credibility to operate. This comes from a wider community of interests and interrelated connections that an external advisor is part of and may be better able to read or relate to. Reputational damage from unfortunate, even unintended, outcomes can be critical to the business's survival if not prosperity.

The general picture over the past five years from research undertaken by the author is that firms continue to improve in compliance terms but find it more difficult to develop a robust governance culture and build effective relationships with stakeholders that add value and recognise the significance of being a good corporate citizen. This is a complex dilemma that can translate into major reputational risk and suboptimal performance at all levels. Addressing governance, ethics, and culture requires a sophisticated response and detailed engineering.

Looking both inside and outside is part of being a healthy and mature organisation. Involving others in this process only deepens and enriches the value. The process of gaining external input only adds diversity and resilience. The benefits far outweigh any concerns of risking upsetting the applecart or breaking confidentiality. One is partly the point; the second is unlikely. Trust, of course, is essential and so is the demonstration of added value. External evaluation itself needs evaluation.

Stakeholder Participation *Stakeholder* has become a term used to identify those who are affected by an organisation's actions or have a relevant interest in them. It is a wider group than shareholders but does include them.

The stakeholder participation process:

- Identifies and understands stakeholders, their capacity to engage, and their views and expectations
- Identifies, develops, and implements appropriate, robust, and balanced engagement strategies, plans, and modes of engagement for stakeholders
- Facilitates understanding, learning, and improvement of the organisation

- Establishes ways for stakeholders to be involved in decisions that will improve overall performance
- Builds the capacity of internal stakeholders and supports building capacity for external stakeholders to engage
- Addresses conflicts or dilemmas among different stakeholder expectations[22]

Part of corporate governance is understanding and paying proper attention to the impacts of the organization's actions on a wide range of stakeholders and to formalise an interaction and reporting process.

CONCLUSION

Governance could be viewed on its own or as part of a wider GRC (Governance, Risk and Compliance) structure, with all parts working together. Compliance sits alongside governance as part of this GRC framework and the staff involved need to share an understanding of the key issues of all areas. This links governance with ethics and culture.

GRC is connected by:

- The direction, values, and strategy of the company
- Corporate culture
- Ethics

and is underpinned by:

- Measurement and evaluation systems
- Education and training

A useful summary framework is shown in Figure 6.1. This sees governance as part of building an overall corporate culture and system of controls. The emphasis is on the whole company. Using all of these principles together, a company needs to develop a coherent governance culture that reaches to all parts of the organisation. This determines how effective the culture can be and also how the organisation is viewed from the outside by investors, potential customers, and regulators.

REVIEW: THE STATE OF CORPORATE GOVERNANCE

The Resources Governance Index (RGI) has been designed and led by the author and is calculated from 2008/2009 to the present. It is now

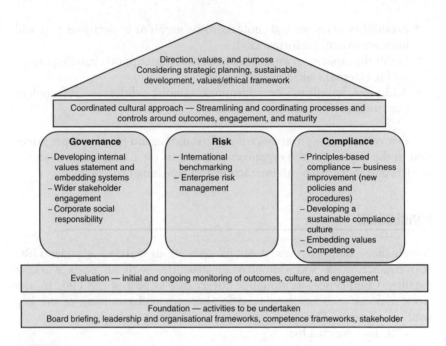

Direction, values, and purpose
Considering strategic planning, sustainable
development, values/ethical framework

Coordinated cultural approach — Streamlining and coordinating processes and
controls around outcomes, engagement, and maturity

Governance	Risk	Compliance
– Developing internal values statement and embedding systems – Wider stakeholder engagement – Corporate social responsibility	– International benchmarking – Enterprise risk management	– Principles-based compliance — business improvement (new policies and procedures) – Developing a sustainable compliance culture – Embedding values – Competence

Evaluation — initial and ongoing monitoring of outcomes, culture, and engagement

Foundation — activities to be undertaken
Board briefing, leadership and organisational frameworks, competence frameworks, stakeholder

FIGURE 6.1 Framework of Governance, Risk, and Compliance

renamed the Ethics Foundation Governance Health Index (EFGHI) and is produced in conjunction with the Ethics Foundation (who offer the Ethics Mark) and Edinburgh University Business School. This index measures companies against the core principles of good governance and is not jurisdiction-specific or based on one country's governance code. The model is broad based and integrates aspects of compliance alongside corporate culture, organisation, and community impact. This is a complex subject, and one strength of the compound model is its inherent complexity and interconnectivity. Governance does not have one simple or direct measure.

We have found remarkably consistent themes.

The Governance Gap between Compliance and Performance

Our research indicates the appearance of a mismatch between the public projection of good governance standards and the internal and external implementation of the core principles in practise.

This fault-line, often between board or central functions and the front line, is concerning because it can become only too apparent in times of stress, and public perceptions of disjunction only serve to continue to undermine trust, leadership, and resolution. We see this as the distance between often high compliance scores in the EFGHI and much less sure performances in measures of internal capacity and external commitment.

There seems to be a small cadre of firms that do score consistently well and these are drawn from a variety of sectors and jurisdictions. The companies that consistently score highly in all categories are:

- GlaxoSmithKline
- Unibail-Rodamco
- BNP Paribas
- Telecom Italia
- InterContinental
- Iberdrola
- Rio Tinto
- Billiton
- HSBC
- AXA
- ENI
- CRH

For many other firms, however, there seems to be a worrying intransigence towards deeper, more important issues of corporate culture, commitment, and engagement.

Superficiality in business is dangerous—it provides a false sense of security and may reveal to any regulator or analyst or, indeed as we have seen, any press or public enquiry a cursory attitude to the core purposes of governance and compliance. Ticking off a checklist cannot be a sensible way of doing governance in any circumstance.

Companies with high compliance scores, which suggest serious and concerted board focus in this area, and good intentions in terms of external image, are undermined by poorer scores in the other categories, showing that these intentions may not translate into a sound governance culture throughout the organisation. The need to embed values and behaviours is clear.

Mediocrity Is Prevalent

Many corporations we've looked at seem content with poor levels of governance performance overall. This is disappointing because these results seem consistent from year to year using our multiple RGI measures. This is true in internal measures of governance, organisation, and culture and also in external community, environmental, and wider social impact measures. This is found in large corporations that are high profile as well as medium-sized companies.

It is true that in all sectors, and most noticeably in financial services, compliance has improved rapidly over the past four years. By 2012, nearly all major corporations were scoring highly in these measures, but this is deceptive. Compliance with (the principles of) Codes of Governance is by definition a precarious measure because these codes are merely minimum standards. Companies are measuring against the weakest. To add to this, comply-and-explain philosophies typical of many jurisdictions give the organisation a way out and, for many who want to, the ability to opt out from full disclosure. This is often expressed in chairpersons' statements in a bland and unconvincing way.

Going along with the crowd is also a missed opportunity to generate a competitive edge. The potential to gain real value from improving governance is missed when an organisation chooses to operate at the level of industry benchmark or minimum regulatory standards.

We suspect that these boards may just not be fully grasping their responsibilities and the potential positive bottom-line impact of good governance. Governance could seem to be a passing fashion, a sideline in response to recent negative headlines, and a "nice to have" but maybe not really necessary. Yet the core direction, values, and behaviour of a company are central to governance and governance is central to business success and will always be.

Governance Is Seen as a Cost, Not an Opportunity

We are continually facing a barrier to progress in governance and this barrier is the *business case*. It is understandable that investment (or review and reengineering) cannot be on the basis of trust and belief in the advantages of good governance alone. We have therefore commissioned research this year into the connection between governance and financial performance.

Without prejudicing results, this academic study by a major business school tested many variables against the EFGHI results and found that there is a correlation between good governance (as measured by the EFGHI) and long-term return on assets. The connection with shorter term profitability was much less clear.

There are several surveys into the relationship between governance and financial performance using the EFGHI data. These have indicated some connection, but this study in 2012 in conjunction with Edinburgh University Business School is more detailed and reliable, based on the UK FTSE 100. The study is careful to establish that the connection is not direct and is not necessarily causal.

It may well be that the holistic nature of the Index gives a better fix on governance than other, more simplistic measures but that, on the other hand, its breadth brings into the picture many variables that impinge on the regression calculations. It does seem that governance pays.

We hope that this contribution will help to make the business case for sound and effective governance and help to remove the barrier to a conversation about deeper and further embedding and development.

Community Engagement Is Undervalued

Engagement with outside partners, stakeholders, and the wider community is often seen as a bureaucratic or expensive add-on and not a driver of authenticity and well-rounded, transformational change. We have generally seen poor scores in the categories concerned with community engagement and an unwillingness to be open to external evaluation (as reflected in our bonus data). Companies may also see industry leadership and subscribing to international standards as non-core.

We have seen scores in these areas decline as scores in compliance rise. Are firms becoming more selfish in times of difficulty? Is this a rational response?

We discovered through further research in this area, with the same business school, a connection with the apparently softer measures of commitment (ex-environmental data that is variably reported) within the governance suite of measures and financial performance.

Being more committed to *corporate social responsibility* (CSR) appears to benefit a company through improved productivity and higher market value. This suggests that the cost of investing in CSR has the potential ROI (return on investment) of higher market value and higher revenue; in essence CSR becomes a company asset with intrinsic value, even if not immediately recognised or measurable.

In today's society, it is widely recognised that for a company, engaging in a formal CSR effort indicates that it has an influential marketing tool by which it can establish and shape its socially responsible image, distinguish itself in highly competitive markets, and gain a competitive edge with a good reputation of caring for society.[23] In today's business environment, corporations that remain profitable and last are those that can keep good relations with their key operating counterparties and build and maintain their good reputations.[24]

The EFGHI research assesses the value of some of these supposed extras. This only serves to strengthen the value of a broad index and validity of including external impact and community contribution dimensions of responsible corporate citizenship.

Intent Is Key

Our Index is very sensitive to proxies for motivation, values, and drivers of change. We are trying to divine the direction of intent of company's senior management and the ethics and spirit of the company as a whole. New regulations place great emphasis on boards considering the spirit of the rules rather than just the letter. *Intent is key to culture.* Many of the reports picking over the failings of 2008 conclude that the behavioural drivers are more significant in success or disaster than organisational or process points.

Our research found certain dimensions of culture, for example, salary range (between CEO pay and average pay), have a particular influence on governance and on financial performance. The overall trend suggests that the higher the salary spread, the lower the overall EFGHI score; that is, stronger corporate governance appears to be directly correlated with tighter salary spreads (within a 90% confidence interval).

With the international, cross-jurisdictional sample of the five companies with the highest overall EFGHI scores, three of them ranked in the 90th percentile for salary spread numbers; of the five companies with the lowest overall EFGHI scores, three ranked in the bottom 25th percentile for salary spread numbers. It may be that the relationship is not causal—we cannot easily test that—but a lesser salary spread seems to be an indicator or proxy for a more integrated and joined-up culture.

In the current economic climate, CEO compensation has been scrutinised as a leading indicator of sound corporate governance. There is a public perception that with CEO salaries there have been rewards for failure and that senior management rewards are disproportionate to the average employee salary. Some countries have sought to regulate compensation, especially in financial services.

How to Raise Standards

The following suggests new standards or amendments to existing standards:

A. Leadership
   1. Boards should be specific and transparent about the competences necessary for the board to work effectively and the contribution provided by each board member. A competence matrix should appear in the Annual Report and Accounts.
   2. The NED selection and induction process should be publically reported.
   3. The criteria for independence should be clear and published in the Annual Report and Accounts.
   4. Chairperson should receive mentoring and be externally evaluated annually by an external party that is not the auditor. Chairpersons are leaders of their industry and need to demonstrate that leadership as well as welding and running an effective senior team.
B. Effectiveness
   1. Boards should attach to all meeting agendas a pre-agreed structured questioning that allows for difficult issues to be raised.
   2. Management information should be audited biannually to ensure board reports are valid and credible and that board decisions are effectively disseminated to all concerned, regularly monitored, and followed up by the board after an agreed reporting period.

3. Boards and all board committees should meet at least every two months.
4. Remuneration for NEDs should be a national standard, may be £25,000 for three days a month, and any exceptions explained in the Annual Report and Accounts.
5. Compliance officers should attend all main board meetings and have unlimited access to a named NED.
6. The training provided by external parties should be reported and evaluated. This should include compliance face-to-face training beyond simple updates or email circulars.

C. Accountability
1. Accountability and external relations—boards should be clear who their stakeholders are in the Annual Report and Accounts.
2. Boards should make clear the purpose of the company in the Annual Report and Accounts, its exact role in the wider community, and its economic impact/outcomes and environmental responsibilities.
Note: This will require a statement of desired outcomes and exact measures of outcome.
3. Boards should set out publicly with rationale their values in the Annual Report and Accounts, their risk appetite, and how they measure and support corporate culture.
4. Boards should seek to use standardised measures of reporting community and environmental commitment.

D. Engagement
1. Boards should specify and illustrate in the Annual Report and Accounts how they conduct ongoing stakeholder engagement.
2. Salary structures should be transparently designed to reflect the values and outcomes stated earlier. All remuneration devices should be declared and explained so that they can be reasonably understood and compared by a non-expert reader.
3. Boards need to demonstrate how no director should be involved in deciding his or her own remuneration.
4. Salary spread should be reported annually.

E. Reporting and evaluation
1. Comply or explain—it is too easy to provide simple or banal explanations for noncompliance with existing governance code standards. Noncompliance should be on an *exceptional* basis only.
2. Detailed explanations should appear in the main body of the Annual Report and Accounts and not just in the chairperson's statement. They should be supported by external, non-auditor, opinion. Explanations should include examples or illustrations of why compliance would be onerous and not effective. A timescale for reverting to normal reporting should be given in every instance. Explanations should be reasonably understandable to non-expert readers.

Boards should be open to external evaluation once every three years and not by and auditor, with the summary in the Annual Report and Accounts.

It is interesting to see if these standards will be raised internationally. Companies, of course, can raise their own standards voluntarily.

ENDNOTES

1. FSA, *The Failure of the Royal Bank of Scotland: Financial Services Authority Board Report* (London: FSA, Dec. 12, 2011).
2. BBC, *Andrew Marr Show,* Prime Minister interview (Jan. 8, 2012).
3. Mirror and Aviva CEOs.
4. FSA, *A Review of Corporate Governance in UK Banks and Other Financial Industry Entities: Final Recommendations* (London: FSA, 2009).
5. Cadbury report, *The Financial Aspects of Corporate Governance* (1992), http://www.icaew.com/~/media/corporate/files/library/subjects/corporate%20governance/financial%20aspects%20of%20corporate%20governance.ashx.
6. D. Higgs, *Review of the Role and Effectiveness of Non-executive Directors* (London: The Stationery Office, 2003).
7. MAS 22.11.11.
8. MAS, *Code of Corporate Governance* (Singapore: MAS, May 2, 2012).
9. FRC, UK Governance Code 2010, Preface, para 7.
10. Ibid., p. 4.
11. *Sunday Times* 1.1.12.
12. FSA, *A Review of Corporate Governance in UK Banks and Other Financial Industry Entities: Final Recommendations* (London: FSA, Nov. 26, 2009, para 3.6).
13. D. Jackman et al., *Resources Governance Index 2009* (London: Resources Global Professionals, 2009).
14. FRC, UK Corporate Governance Code 2012, Preface.
15. UK Corporate Governance Code 2012, Preface.
16. FSA, Jackman (2002).
17. UK Corporate Governance Code 2010, B2.
18. Ibid., B7.
19. Revisions to FRC Guidance on Audit Committees: Non-Audit Services (July 2010).
20. Ibid.
21. Direct Government UK.
22. AccountAbility, AA1000: Accountability Principles Standard 2008, http://www.accountability.org/images/content/0/7/074/AA1000APS%202008.pdf.
23. C. Lin, H. Yang, and D. Liou, "The Impact of Corporate Social Responsibility on Financial Performance: Evidence from Business in Taiwan," *Technology in Society* 31(2009): 56–63.
24. P. Beurden and T. Gossling, "The Worth of Values: A Literature Review on the Relation between Corporate Social and Financial Performance," *Journal of Business Ethics* 82(2008): 407–424.

CHAPTER 7

Outcomes[1]

For the old Man—and 'tis believed by all
That many and many a day he thither went,
And never lifted up a single stone.
There, by the Sheepfold, sometimes was he seen
Sitting alone, or with his faithful Dog,
Then old, beside him, lying at his feet.
The length of full seven years, from time to time,
He at the building of this Sheepfold wrought,
And left the work unfinished when he died.
       —William Wordsworth (1770–1850), "Michael—a pastoral
                                                      poem"

This is the beginning of stage 5 of the General Model of Regulation and Compliance.

WHY IS THIS STEP UP SO SIGNIFICANT?

Outcome changes everything. The introduction of this perspective should be taken very seriously by compliance, as it is a set of concepts that is revolutionary in itself and changes the fundamentals in regulation. The key changes are that outcomes-focused regulation and compliance:

1. Introduces a new set of criteria for judging the success of compliance
2. Requires compliance to use new forms of measurement within the business
3. Provides an additional perspective for making compliance decisions that necessitates compliance occupying a more strategic position

The key to the change is in effect looking from the other end of the telescope, at results and effects instead of processes and inputs. The shift is from the internal to the external: to consumers, potential consumers, and wider society at large.

This is not to say that prior emphases on capital, ethics, culture, governance, and conduct risk are less important, but this adds a new layer to the cake or an additional thread to be wound into the warp and weft of compliance. It is a transformational move because the different perspective it provides changes the way the other threads operate and can be viewed. The whole enterprise of regulation and compliance is now on a new foundation.

The FCA has gone to pains to jolt the industry to understand that outcome is something different and worth taking notice of. Why else would FCA say that what matters is what outcomes are achieved for consumers, not whether a firm complies with the rules? PRA explains that firms should manage:

> ... in line with ... spirit and intended outcome—not managing the business only to the letter, or gaming the rules.[2]

So it is not that processes and internal controls don't matter, but they are not *all* that matters. Consequently, it is no longer a watertight defence to claim that compliance has the appropriate systems and controls in place and religiously recorded how it acted ethically with good culture, and why the governance decisions were made as they were. *Compliance actually has to get the right result, too.*

Deciding what is this right result is difficult and depends greatly on time horizon. What seems good in the short term may well not pass muster years later, or vice versa. The need to decide about desirable results brings the prospect of increasing retrospective judgment by regulatory authorities. Regulation will be judging, even second-guessing, compliance judgments for an indefinite period after those decisions have been taken. Compliance can therefore never rest easy.

Consequently the quality of individual and collective judgments really matters; outcome evaluation and measurement is not just a matter of mechanics, ticking the right boxes and filing returns on time. It will be a continuous process of checking what has transpired and how impacts become cumulative and how the various outcomes interact with each other. Aggregated outcome risk is likely to become a new feature of regulatory risk.

Much more skill is required to bring the outcome into play with existing themes, and working these together will require a huge step up in compliance skill and professionalism. This is indeed a revolution and it is starting now.

WHAT IS OUTCOME?

This is difficult to define. It encompasses all the effects of a financial institution's actions and inactions, behaviours, statements, positions, and influences. These effects may be specific or general, immediate or long term. They may be collective or discrete and firms in the same sector operating similarly may create systemic outcomes. These in turn may be local, national, or international. The scales are infinitely varied.

On whom is the impact? In this context, the primary focus seems to be on financial services consumers and potential consumers, but in fact regulatory concern runs to the wider impacts on the economy and society, including those who may not be your customers. They may be dependents, children, older people, relatives, friends, associates, colleagues, and so forth. The impact may be more diffuse, such as effects of lending policies or interest rates on general levels of confidence, investment, spending, and saving.

We shall speak here of *stakeholders* in financial services firms. It is a rather hackneyed and overused term to mean anyone with a legitimate interest in the activities or decisions of a firm or sector or who may be impacted by the firm's decisions and actions. There is an extensive process of stakeholder identification for any firm to do to understand who its stakeholders are and their interests. This process has little meaning unless it is continuous and involves two-way communication and engagement, especially so that stakeholders can understand and become educated about a firm's operating model, intentions, planned impacts, and prospects. Stakeholders need to be ranked by the materiality of their interest.

The sorts of impacts that might be considered significant by regulators in financial services include:

- Accessibility to funds for housing, especially for first-time buyers
- Willingness to provide credit and finance for small businesses, including start-ups
- Retirement options, their return, and security
- Help for low-paid job-seekers and those in short- and long-term difficulty or debt
- Levels of those who find themselves or chose to be financially excluded
- Accounts to help students and job-seekers
- Levels of confidence and trust in financial services
- Levels of competition and diversity of choice

It is important to note that outcomes can be positive to varying degrees and it is necessary to differentiate between differing levels of good outcomes. Similarly, poor outcomes may not just amount to or be defined as financial loss; they may be loss of opportunity or less-good opportunities, loss of confidence, detrimental effects on dependents and their prospects, a lessening of choice or flexibility, and a fall in status or credit rating. It will emerge over time how these much more intangible impacts will be calculated and weighed.

The outcomes are affected by a wide range of internal policy choices, such as:

1. Credit availability and lending policies
2. Mortgage availability, threshold levels, scoring systems and policies
3. Aggressive nature of charging, especially for overdrafts
4. Attitudes towards vulnerable consumers
5. Cross-subsidies
6. Readiness to repossess housing
7. Profit and charging levels and the balance of benefits
8. Competence and values of staff

The list is in fact infinite. That is why compliance has a new role in deciding what is truly important by way of impact and the internal changes and controls that could be changed to make a meaningful difference.

WHY IS OUTCOME SO IMPORTANT?

Outcome switches the interest from the causes of problems to the results or impacts of problems. This is important for compliance in two ways: first, it places greater emphasis on external stakeholders such as customers rather than the firm or industry (which by contrast can seem inward-looking and self-serving), and second, evaluating outcome introduces a new set of criteria for judging an action or event and assessing how severe it is in regulatory and compliance terms. Outcome does not replace anything that has gone before but it does add a new dimension and in some senses doubles the demands on compliance officers. Introducing outcome-based regulation is not a last resort, although it can be seen as a reaction to the impacts of 2008, but is more properly the next logical step in developing the regulatory panoply and being more effective in delivering a quality compliance.

External: Lessons from 2008   We have witnessed the sinews of our economy and society in the raw since 2008, laid bare in a way almost unprecedented in living memory. We have seen in banking and trading how a few can rig an entire system to secure commercial advantage, and in the process endanger whole economies. Others seem to profit on our high streets but pay negligible tax elsewhere, and governments can pursue ideological agendas while the less fortunate lose livelihoods, education, or prospects of a decent future. Is this all necessary and inevitable?

Arguably the public's sensibilities have been dulled. They have seen nearly every large financial institution come under scrutiny or fail. Would the average person know which banks had been fined? The effects of enforcement in damaging reputation may have been temporarily lost. Have the public therefore become inured and accepting of systemic, cynical arrogance? Public inquiries tell us little. At best we uncover "Murdoch's fork"—a non-choice between incompetence or collusion. Governance clearly doesn't appear to the consumer to be working.

We know the public colluded in the 2008 crash themselves, demanding cheap credit and deifying "the market." The public acceded to the bonus culture by failing to ask serious questions and now accepts, up to a point, that there is a price to pay in terms of austerity, low interest rates, and difficult access to credit. But is this the right price and are the right people paying it? What does this say about our democracy and our values?

Is the industry out of answers? Growth is not sustainable everywhere; debts are still climbing. Banks' internal measures seem superficial—a new ethics code here, an hour's sheep-dip training there is called integrity, a smidgeon of extra reporting is called transparency, and a few new management faces is called cultural change. Hey-presto, you've ticked all the boxes and can carry on with business as usual.

Society finds itself in a difficult place generally. It needs the financial services industry but does not like its position of power. Inequality screams, and there are a lack of options on offer. Where is radical thought? Leadership and intellectual foment is failing from the usual sources. Trust is low all around. We need to start from defining the outcomes we all want, firms and consumers.

Internal: The Need for Greater Direction in Regulation and Compliance In 2004, the author published a paper entitled "Does Regulation Make It Worse?"[3] The thesis was that having no sense of intended outcome left regulation, and by definition compliance, rudderless. It might then do all kinds of things without due cause or sound justification. It might also create unintended consequences that are more troubling than the failure the rule or intervention was designed to address. In other words, without a test of desirable outcome it is impossible for regulators to know exactly what to do or for the industry, consumers, and politicians to judge whether they are doing a decent job. The same applies to compliance.

The point is this: regulation and compliance is not an end in itself and must be for some purpose or desired result. For a long period, regulators have tended to solve immediate problems without considering the long-term strategic intent; that is, what sort of socioeconomic system do we want and what social benefits or goods do we want financial services to deliver? These have been regarded as political questions. But increasingly, and particularly since 2008, when it became apparent in President Obama's words that "Wall Street was affecting Main Street," politicians have been requiring regulators to consider and measure the impacts of their interventions, although continuing to set direction and general parameters. The same discipline applies to compliance functions. They need to calculate the effect their firm's actions will have on a wide range of customer types and on existing and potential future customers, as well as society and the economy at large.

Outcome analysis may not tell compliance exactly what to do, but it adds another point of reference to the triangulation process and balances the push of process regulation with important pull factors. This directs regulation and compliance in a more efficient and useful way.

Measuring Outcome

Measuring outcome is not the same as service levels or customer experience or even treating customers fairly (TCF). Six *consumer outcomes* were used to set the framework for TCF. Although the indicators published in 2007[4] are still useful pointers towards producing suitable outcomes, these indicators are still inwardly focussed and the TCF initiative is not the total universe of outcomes.

Look at Table 7.1 to compare some examples of these categories.

Regulators are unlikely to dictate material outcomes as they are too firm–customer–product specific and they also would not want to pigeonhole firms into producing one kind of result for every client. So it is necessary to set out your own criteria in the following way.

1. Define the sensitive outcome areas for a range of products or services the typical customer groups considering financial circumstances, priorities, values, and needs.

   This requires compliance to judge the most significant outcomes from a long possible list, such as:

TABLE 7.1   Service levels and customer outcomes.

Service Levels	Customer Experience	TCF	Outcomes
Calls answered per hour	Call response time; questions taken seriously, dealt with competently	Resolution of query one-touch or confirmation of agreed timescale	Consumers better informed and better able to secure outcomes desired
New business targets met	Courteous, helpful, no small print, no unexpected penalties, charges, or exclusions	Suitability, persistency, not overinflated profit or margins	Products deliver life outcomes expected, allowing flexibility for changing circumstances
Percent market share increased	Choice of product options Attractive rates	Fair dealing for existing customers Wake-up packs	No unintended consequences or dislocation
Complaints lowered	Listened to; explanations and apologies clear	Root causes analysed Written confirmation sent	Errors are corrected without other error Losses restored Consumer learning
Investment level delivered	Access to more advantageous products	Investment security Due diligence, suitability check	Investment delivers social benefits or ethical values?

- Impact of decisions on access to housing, especially for young, vulnerable, infirm, and first-time buyers
- Ability to start up small businesses or boost employment in the area
- Flexibility of retirement options versus potential risks
- Reducing long-term debt
- Inclusivity for all groups

2. Calibrate each outcome with appropriate measures (e.g., numbers of first-time buyers awarded a mortgage). The likelihood of that level being achieved over time gives a best-fit line, much like determining probability for risk mapping, as does the same arithmetic for the converse, say repossessions. The zone between the lines provides the acceptable outcome distribution.

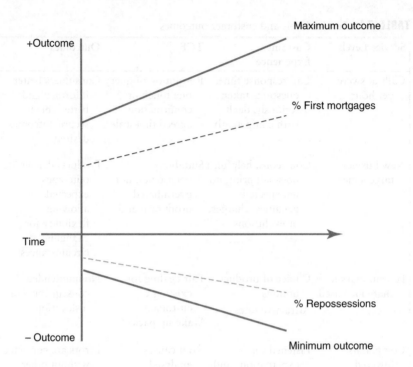

Developing numerical indicators of acceptable levels is an emerging area but it is necessary for firms or industry bodies to develop their own set of benchmark standards. The regulator will be looking to see that these measures are:

- Appropriate to the risks and nature of the business
- Properly explained and documented
- Applied consistently across the firm
- Used in product design to make a difference
- Applied in compliance testing
- Agreed, reviewed, and monitored by boards
- In line with risk appetite
- Fully embedded in compliance practices
- Understood by key staff
- Constantly or regularly reviewed

3. Decide how to evaluate success. Standards can be based on other sources of recognised expertise and international norms, where appropriate. These may come from outside the industry, such as the new ISO international standards (see Chapter 8) and can be tracked through a development matrix.

DEVELOPMENT MATRIX

There is no one magic measure of outcome, so a development matrix approach can be used, bringing together many different measures based, for instance, on the principles of a sustainable community given previously. These show the outcomes of a company or even a sector. They can be very useful for companies in financial services where their impacts can be so widespread.

In Table 7.2, the products or services are listed down the columns and the rows show differing styles of compliance or compliance culture. Taken together the matrix supplies a map of an individual firm's progress and outcome delivery. The matrix will evolve over time and specific measures can then be added.

Development or maturity matrices are used in many contexts, such as sustainability, to show growth and also to profile the current governance health of the company. It is possible to fix numerical measures to all of these. This system also offers regulators a framework for comparing firms and categorising them by their compliance commitment and culture.

Regulators are unlikely to tell firms or sectors what they see as material outcomes or the ways of addressing these. Their argument is that outcomes are too firm–customer–product specific and they also would not want to pigeonhole firms into producing one kind of result for every client. In fact, the approach is designed to encourage competition and diversity of results. The effect of process regulation has been standardised products that are easier for compliance to control and justify but that limit the range of options open to the consumer.

An outcome-based approach frees the firm from producing standard solutions and following a formulaic pattern of advice giving. Rather, with the focus on outcome, so long as the lifestyle and results the customer wanted are realised, then how you got there is secondary. This allows firms to tailor their offerings in a much more individual way. This has two important implications:

1. Firms can become differentiated from competitors by the *quality* of their advice and their approach to compliance.
2. Financial advice and services should end up being more suitable.

   Compliance is key in this as it has new roles to play:

   - Determining the new kinds of offering that can be made within the boundaries of the rules.
   - Evaluating and monitoring the short-, medium-, and long-term impact on various customer groups.

TABLE 7.2 Service and outcome delivery.

Product/Service	Key Issues	Outcomes from Minimal Compliance Regime	Outcomes from Conservative Tickbox Compliance	Outcomes from Business-Led Compliance	Outcomes from a Confident Values-Led Culture
Mortgages	Access to lending for vulnerable groups and commitment under pressure	Basic products; low persistency, dislocation in housing market, repossession aggressive	Only safe customers eligible on points system; disempowerment of community Homelessness or parents' home	Tailored products, wider range, competitive rates, greater choice and flexibility	Customer needs met, even when nonstandard, same offer to existing customers, ethical options
Insurance	Premiums not prohibitive, reasonable conditions, effective competition	Targeting high margin Poor service and follow-up, price following	Tickbox approval, web supermarkets Hidden exclusions in small print	Marginal markets tailored to specific hard-to-meet needs, for example, health	Flexible payments, periods, etc. No small print Open conditions
Deposits	Range of services, security, rates	Limited number of standard accounts	High level of KYC Low interest Inflexible	More creative rates and services	Something different in services, charging, access

- Changing the focus of monitoring from process to outcome contributes crucially to the viability of new kinds of product, how advice is offered, and how charges, terms and conditions, and policies are applied.
- Reducing the overall cost of compliance and operations.

OUTCOMES IN SINGAPORE REGULATION

In Singapore, MAS has through its "Effective Tenets of Regulation" (2010) framework set out an intention to focus on outcomes.

These tenets include:

Tenet 1: "Outcome Focused" requires MAS to uphold sound regulation of a high standard and to give consideration to all of the six Tenets concurrently. Where the Tenets do not pull in the same direction, to exercise appropriate judgement as to how and in what measure the Tenets should be applied in the particular circumstances of each new regulation so that good regulatory outcomes can be achieved.

Tenet 2: "Shared Responsibility" acknowledges that regulation alone is insufficient to deliver good regulatory outcomes. In many areas, good outcomes are most effectively achieved with the MAS, financial institutions, investors and consumers each taking on specific responsibilities for and shared ownership of regulatory objectives and outcomes.

Practice will identify, often in dialogue with the regulator, what is acceptable outcome.

How Supervision Is Changing in the UK

There is a significant increase in the resources devoted to the supervision of high-impact firms, and in particular to high-impact and complex banks, with an increase in the frequency of comprehensive risk reviews from a maximum of three to a maximum of two years, and less for firms facing particularly risky issues.

- A shift in supervisory style from focusing on systems and processes to focusing on key business outcomes and risks and on the sustainability of business models and strategies. This shift will imply a greater willingness to vary capital and liquidity requirements or to intervene more directly if FCA perceives that specific business strategies are creating undue risk to the bank itself or to the wider system.
- A shift in the approach to the assessment of approved persons, with a focus on technical skills as well as probity.

- An increase in resources devoted to sectoral and firm comparator analysis, enabling the FCA to better identify firms that are outliers in terms of risks and business strategies and to identify emerging sector-wide trends that may create systemic risk.
- Investments in specialist skills (e.g., in the analysis of liquidity risks), with supervisory teams able to draw on enhanced central expert resources.
- A much more intensive analysis of information relating to key risks, with, for instance, far more detailed information requirements relating to liquidity.

OUTCOMES AND ENFORCEMENT

The development of regulatory thinking is set out in the General Model and each stage also provides the basis for new offences, new scales of fines, and forms of enforcement.

The emergence of outcome as a new measurement criterion allows for a significant rise in enforcement levels because the offence can be seen as being against the entire community, society, or system. If a firm infringes against a technical rule, the fine may be limited to the dimension of the incompetence or negligence or fraud and so amount to a few tens of thousands, for example. If a firm is seen to infringe an ethical principle such as integrity or fairness, the sanction can be proportionally higher because the fault is seen to be more fundamental. If a poor outcome is caused across a wide customer base having a deleterious effect on life-chances, opportunities, and prosperity, then the scale of a fine could be almost limitless. We have seen such an upscaling in the fines levied against HSBC, Standard Chartered, and the many PPI cases. In all cases compliance may not have had its eye on the end result, but rather contented itself in fussing about technical details.

Action

A useful check for compliance and the board could be the following eight questions:

1. How have you designed your governance structures and processes to ensure that consumer outcomes are central to your strategy and decision making?
2. How are you ensuring that decisions consider all material stakeholders and are fairly taken?
3. How do you ensure no one stakeholder has an unfair outcome or degree of influence in determining outcomes?

4. How do you encourage the free flow of ideas, contributions, and information into the outcome-centred compliance?
5. How easily can any relevant interested parties find outcome statements and evaluations and how can they provide feedback?
6. How do you reduce barriers to progress and bureaucracy to allow innovation, appropriate risk, diversity, and prosperity?
7. How do you consciously develop a mind-set that values the outcomes for all sections of the community, vulnerable customers, and the generations that follow us?
8. Do you measure realistic and practical outcome expectations?

This is just the start of a journey that can revise all that compliance considers and the information the board receives. It is a fundamentally new set of criteria.

CONCLUSION

Outcome requires an analysis of impact. It is also creating a new direction for compliance. Compliance that starts with an understanding of what is being achieved, in terms of wider society, utility, and service might be better placed to begin a useful journey than one that jumps in the middle and thrashes around until it appears to float.

There are some very useful principles of outcome that need to be widely understood and developed.[5] These are complex terms with complex impacts affecting all of us. To understand how these all interact requires a higher degree of sophistication than designing and running systems and controls at arm's length. This is an inside-out activity, concerned as much about internal efficiency as the concentric circles of interdependence—we could say of the wider community.

Finally, this element, like all the other elements covered in Part II, influences the competences that compliance needs and alters the role because outcomes:

- Allow a more direct connection between compliance and the bottom line performance and reputational risk.
- Give more scope for compliance to act strategically.
- Require compliance to become involved in board and senior management decisions (i.e., upstream in the decision-making process).
- Empower compliance to explore new and innovative methods of operation that contribute directly to competitive advantage.
- Provide direct relationship with regulatory priorities that was lacking under a governance and cultural perspective.

Chapter 8 continues the focus on outcomes but at a higher level of resolution and in the context of the broad sweep of compliance development.

The shifts of role inherent in the new approaches of Chapters 4–7 as well as Chapter 8 provide a platform for professionalism that is explored in Chapter 9.

ENDNOTES

1. An earlier version of this chapter appeared in *Business Compliance* 6 (2014).
2. Bank of England, Prudential Regulation Authority, *The PRA's Approach to Banking Supervision* (London: The Stationery Office, 2012), http://www.bankofengland.co.uk/publications/Documents/other/pra/bankingappr1210.pdf.
3. David Jackman, "Does Regulation Make It Worse?," *Journal of Financial Regulation and Compliance* 12, No. 2 (2004): 106–110.
4. FSA, *Treating Customers Fairly: Culture* (London: FSA, 2007).
5. BS8904, *Sustainable Communities 2011*; ISO 37101, *Sustainable and Resilient Communities (under Development)*; ISO 37120/151, *Smart Cities*, International Standards Organisation, forthcoming.

Three

Purpose

Compliance and regulation is a hope for something better—it has purpose. Compliance may not be delivering quite yet, but by understanding the underlying processes we can steer compliance in a positive direction.

In this part we consider:

1. *Community*—overall purpose
2. *Corporate faith*—how purpose is translated into business drivers
3. *Corporate maturity*—developing maturity and the processes of change

How compliance understands purpose will determine compliance's performance in the foreseeable future and its survival as a profession.

Although ethics, culture, governance, outcome, and community have emerged as logical additions to the regulation and compliance toolkit, they need to be understood as operating together to:

1. Create an infrastructure that allows stages 4 and 5 to be sufficiently embedded.
2. Provide an extended toolkit to allow new challenges to be faced.
3. Explain the core processes that drive compliance performance.
4. Offer a framework for improving performance.
5. Improve the credibility and standing of compliance.
6. Offer a sense of overall purpose.
7. Ensure that compliance will become a profession.

Recently, there has been a tendency to see compliance under the umbrella term *governance, risk, and compliance* (GRC). This correctly recognizes the need for a joined-up approach but fails to identify the processes and structures that operationalize and justify this connection. Part III aims to provide that framework.

Community

The best things any mortal hath are those which every mortal shares.

—T. Arthur Leonard (1864–1948)

What makes outcome so difficult to identify and to pin down is the lack of an *endgame*. What is the overall purpose of compliance? What is the point? All that has gone before hopefully underlines the unlikelihood of a specific end result. There is not going to be a finite point when all regulation and compliance has achieved all that it set out to do, but there might be a path that can be identified that takes compliance forward on a reasonably sound footing for the foreseeable future, able to deal with most things that could be thrown at it and, crucially, in control of its own destiny.

The sustainable path or place of equilibrium is an industry in balance with its community, an industry that is providing more or less the services and products expected and needed by the community, enabling it to achieve its objectives, to prosper, and to provide sustainable wealth and wellbeing to all its members fairly. This equilibrium also involves being resilient to external shocks, adaptable to change, and alive to new opportunities. It is also smart and efficient in the way the community operates and financial services are delivered within it. This, of course, is an ideal and will vary from community to community and from time to time; but if we can become better at defining what a community needs and desires, then the overall outcome of financial services is better adjusted and connected to its end users.

This is essentially a holistic perspective and the widest form of consideration of outcome, but it does provide the most reliable and justifiable position for shaping and evaluating compliance and the intervention of regulation. It is a perspective that is emerging already and more strongly in public comment on the future of banking and financial services. This requires a more sophisticated analysis than the more mechanical level of outcome in Chapter 7. We may wish to regard this as a further, and possibly final, stage in the General Model—stage 6.

IMPORTANCE OF COMMUNITY

Community can be seen as the ultimate point of reference for a company or a sector; it provides definition for its role and justification for its existence. If community needs and expectations change, the sector must reflect these changing needs or the companies will lose their legitimacy and fail to be supported and patronised. Companies can also help to shape communities' perceptions of needs through marketing—in 2008, that contributory or escalating factor was the widespread recasting of consumer desires as needs, boosted by financial services marketing of relatively cheap credit and apparently affordable mortgages. This distortion of the community's collective requirements for financial services is usually short-lived and an equilibrium is re-found usually through the operation of fiscal and monetary policies, reflecting a more sober will.

However, community has ultimate sway in determining the form of financial services that is necessary and the patterns of behaviour that are acceptable. Community exercises control through:

- Providing the legitimacy to carry out business through issuing a licence to practice by regulatory or governmental authorities, reflecting the community's will or interests.
- Consumer purchasing decisions—community members will not, ideally, purchase products and services that are injurious to the wider purposes or the community, financial services being a service function.
- Investment decisions—communities will, through direct public and indirect private investment choices, elect to invest in those vehicles that best suit broader aims.

Those services and firms that are sustainable and best-adjusted to community aims will survive and prosper while those ill-adjusted will not.

ROLE OF COMPANIES

The purpose of a company is much more complex than shareholder return. Companies play a role in the wider society and economy by doing something. They add value by creating and consuming a wide range of products or materials, manufacturing, servicing, collecting and distributing, trading, entertaining, educating, or building for the future. They buy from and support a ring of suppliers, large and small. There is in effect an outcome or series of outcomes, all of which have some use, meaning, or worth. Very few companies could get away with producing something nobody needs or values.

The role companies play goes further, to providing employment, which in turn generates salaries and benefits for families, which in turn again allows for purchasing from local stores and producers and thereby supports a penumbra of other businesses, their employees, and families. Employment also gives individuals and their families benefits in terms of a sense of identity, worth, and confidence, it provides economic and social stability, and by creating environments and architectures companies shape the built fabric and natural landscape around us. This is both a contribution in the present and a heritage for the future. Companies can act in this sense to aid sustainability or to undermine it.

Companies are hubs for local communities, generators of wealth—which is fed into the local economy—as well as part of the social fabric, a focus for meeting, exchanging ideas, innovation, participation, and sometimes even celebration. Companies create activity, pay taxes and rates, affect local democracy, and contribute to local causes. They are part of the scenery, the sense of place. Companies, whether they are aware of it or not, have a purpose in playing a part as corporate citizens, with at least the same responsibilities as individuals. This line of reasoning may not resonate with some companies, but it needs to so they can start to define their purpose beyond pure monetary profit.

This is a very solid purpose and role and brings with it a sense of identity and real responsibilities. If a company decides to streamline a process and therefore make a number of employees redundant, that decision has a spiral of effect on local wealth, businesses, families, services, and future prospects. Its purpose has in some respects been damaged, but companies rarely see it in that way. Some would say all of this is too complicated, but reality is complicated and the effects of company actions can be just as significant as policy changes by government, or at least local government, and such changes would be open to a high level of public scrutiny and debate as well as accountability. No-one would reasonably expect such detailed debate for a normal company decision, unless they were a state concern or involved in a strategic project such as building a new airport, power station, or railway line where the planning process would allow for public engagement. Yet how can companies exercise some level of awareness and engagement about purpose and responsibility while still working effectively?

SOCIAL USEFULNESS OF BANKS

Lord Turner, chairman of the FSA, sparked much debate in 2009 about the "social usefulness" of banks.[1] This was a genuine question, which was greatly misunderstood (possibly deliberately by some in the industry) and re-translated as questioning the entire role of banks. What he perhaps meant to do was to stimulate a discussion about what role society and communities want financial services to perform and the social and economic "goods" or outcomes we can trust it will deliver.

The rational part of the discussion ran into the sand as it was too soon after the crises of 2008 but has been revived many times since. In particular, it will become highly impactful in the legislation aimed at implementing *ring fencing*, which puts in place a distinction between retail and wholesale banking. That discussion will result in retail banks having to adopt very different behaviours and strategies than in the past without the consequent rewards and with very different compliance regimes.

The distinction will lie between "utility banking" and riskier investment or "casino banking," which will be allowed to trade on its own account but not in any way that jeopardises the capital of its retail partners or puts at risk retail depositors. These arguments play directly into the sorts of outcomes regulators need to deliver and sit behind what may well emerge as the likely differences in regulatory approaches—one focusing on utility issues, the other investment market issues.

The reason why financial services are the focus of a discussion that could equally be put at the door of pharmaceuticals or energy utilities or broadcasting (and to a lesser extent is, from time to time) is that financial services occupies a unique pivotal role in communities. This is partly in the way it collects and channels resources and also because its behaviour affects the tone and confidence of almost all other sectors that are in some way dependent upon it. It becomes the arbiter of enterprise, determining which schemes will survive and which will fail. And, of course, it has the unique capacity to affect all the many consumers who rely on the safekeeping, transmission, and investment of money and value.

A range of studies, including the Stieglitz report, sponsored by the French government, on "Gross National Happiness"—as an alternative to Gross National Product (GNP)—have informed an even wider debate on the forms of progress that society should consider. The alternative measures of wealth simply reflect individual awareness of wellbeing and an increased weighing of ethical issues. This determines what we want to see from retailers and suppliers, including financial services suppliers. This trend may simply be a luxury, an expression of an affluent middle class living longer. But changing attitudes affect behaviour and choices. We may decide to tone down our aspirations and work rate in favour of less tangible but more fulfilling ways of spending our time. A recent study suggested the "happiest wage" was £45,000.

The largest global corporations can have more influence than some individual nation states, and their globalised nature can elevate them above and beyond the reach of national regulators and tax authorities. We have seen concerns about Google, Starbucks, and Amazon not paying what appear to be reasonable levels of tax in the countries in which they generate their profitability. The UK Chancellor announced in December 2014 measures to close loopholes on accounting practices that allow profits to be diffused. A so-called "Google tax" has also been proposed in recognition of the growing public disquiet about corporate behaviour and the attitudes and values they reveal. Some consumers may cease patronising certain retailers and products. A foretaste of the power of consumer views about community issues was the boycotting of cheap tee-shirts from high-street stores following the appalling loss of life in Bangladesh when a clothing factory, known to be unsafe, collapsed, killing many workers on low pay. Retailers have had to find new suppliers and issue declarations of good practice in relation to their supply chains and workers' conditions. Community legitimacy is beginning to bite.

ROLE OF COMPLIANCE

Compliance acts for us, society, as much as for the regulator and the firm. Compliance and financial services will be more at rest when it finds its equilibrium with the community around it. Almost all of what has gone before in this book is as a result of disequilibrium between the industry and the rest of society: a *dis-ease*.

Compliance needs to be close to community need. Compliance holds a heavy responsibility possibly too lightly at the moment. Compliance's core job is to ensure, beyond any reasonable doubt, that it understands and makes good the industry's promises to its own wider community. This is vital for the firm's sustainability and the prosperity of the community.

There are five functions compliance could consider to embed a community outcome perspective.

1. Socially responsible financial products and services:
   - Does your firm offer ethical alternatives?
   - Do social and ethical investments and products and services fulfil accurately the conditions of their schemes?
   - Do they comply with their own stated standards?
   - Is reporting transparent, full, and fair?

2. Public accountability and reporting:
   - Is your reporting full and fair against voluntary standards? Including those covering environmental standards?
   - Is your reporting fulfilling your own claims?
   - Is your reporting fulfilling the Stewardship Code?
   - Is your reporting fulfilling the spirit of the Governance Code and regulatory principles?

3. Social and community engagement:
   - How inclusive and rigorous is your stakeholder engagement?
   - Does your engagement follow good process?
   - How can you show this?
   - How can you ensure you have not neglected any significant, neglected, or disadvantaged groups or individuals?
   - How can you show that the results have been incorporated in your operations and strategy?

4. Social investment:
   - How do you develop your community and sector in a mature way to be responsible beyond compliance?
   - How do you lead?
   - How do you educate?
   - How do you ensure the benefits and costs are spread equitably?

5. Specific requirements (e.g., bribery and corruption):
   - How do you demonstrate your compliance, independence, and objectivity at all times?

But these items merely support a community outcomes approach. Understanding the longer term community outcomes must inform compliance input to all aspects of the business from product design, service delivery standards, and conduct risk to customer surveys and reputational management. This focus on community strengthens the case for the more strategic role for compliance. However, compliance needs to be clear about what we mean by community.

DEFINITION OF *COMMUNITY*

Community may be defined thus:

> Community arises from people living, working or being together; gaining mutual benefits from exchange, cooperation or shared interests. Community produces and is strengthened by shared values, common experiences and a sense of identity and belonging.

In addition:

Sustainable and resilient communities have a long-term view of their shared interests taking into account future generations' needs and building in capabilities and capacities to meet potential challenges.[2]

Organisations are structural units within which community develops and shared systems develop. Businesses of all kinds are therefore part of the community and not separate from the community. It is not appropriate to talk about corporate links with the community, community responsibility, or even community engagement as though a firm is somehow separate. Business is functioning as an integral component within the community; it is of the community and the community is of it. The term needs not redefining, but reevaluating.

COMMUNITY PRINCIPLES

So what does community want? Recent work by the author, leading the UK input to international standards, is trying to define what makes a healthy, resilient, sustainable, and smart community. The international standards body, ISO, based in Geneva is running the standards-setting programme that will take many years but that is beginning to present its high-level findings. The intention is to publish a framework document, ISO 37101—Sustainable Development of Communities—in 2015 for consultation. The pre-existing British Standard for community sustainability—BS8904—championed, led, and drafted by the author, interestingly sets out purposes and principles for community that have found their way into the international work. These include:

- *Mutuality*: Understanding how a group of people (community), through cooperation, are able to act for their mutual benefit.
- *Connectedness and sense of place*: Understanding the close interaction between economic, social, and environmental aspects within a distinctive locale or shared interest group with common experiences, values, and cultural traditions.
- *Intracommunity equity*: Improving equity within different communities and groups, and between neighbouring communities (or beyond). This is based on concepts of social justice, and also implies that consumption and production supported in one community should not undermine the ecological, social, and economic basis for other communities to maintain or improve their quality of life.

- *Intergenerational equity:* Equity between different age-groups of people alive today and between present and future generations. Community sustainability involves ensuring that future generations will have the means to achieve a quality of life equal to or better than today's.
- *Prosperous, resilient, and adaptable:* Communities are capable of creating wealth and wellbeing in the long term, and are capable of bouncing back from adverse situations or responding to changing circumstances, including seeking opportunities, investing in building new capabilities, and releasing or enabling reservoirs of knowhow and skills.
- *Shared external relationships:* Open to outside ideas, people, and contributions integrating new and existing links and traditions. For compliance this may seem remote but policy actions and products issued by firms can erode these community aims and have possibly unintended but discriminatory consequences for certain groups who may then bring class actions or undermine the institution's reputation. One obvious and fundamental question of our time comes from the overprotection and favourable treatment given to pensions or retirement options.

Unsustainable production and consumption by today's society paid for by credit could degrade the ecological, social, and economic opportunities for tomorrow's society. Current generations could spend at a higher than sustainable rate and leave the debt for younger generations to pay. This reality is particularly acute in aging societies (e.g., Europe and Japan) where there is considerable purchasing and political power exercised by older groups at the expense (although maybe not consciously) of younger generations in terms of financial products and outcomes. This is reflected in current regulations and the products and services offered by financial institutions, but this may not be sustainable if unemployment, relative poverty, and houselessness in younger groups grows to unacceptable levels. These younger generations will also be funding the national debts built up by their predecessors and the public services strained by the needs of the voting elderly while receiving poorer services themselves and stagnant or even falling incomes. The debate is now active; the role of compliance is to be ready for any number of scenarios that may emerge and to ensure their institution is prepared with inventive solutions.

SUSTAINABLE COMMUNITIES PRINCIPLES—WHAT DO THEY MEAN?[3]

If these principles are the core needs or desires of most communities, compliance must understand better what these principles mean. (See Table 8.1.)

TABLE 8.1 Sustainable communities principles.

Mutuality is derived from the fact that a group of people, through cooperation, are better able to act for their mutual benefit than if acting alone. From this simple but central tenet comes the overarching objective of mutuality: namely, that mutuals seek to benefit their members' quality of life rather than maximize profit.	Respect for all members in the community, irrespective of age, background, physical and social mobility—all are considered and treated with dignity and given the chance to belong and participate. Collective grassroots initiatives (e.g., CICs, credit unions).
Engagement, inclusivity, and accountability: Inclusive participation based on strong democratic principles and good governance—differences are encouraged but are mediated and are resolvable. Accountability to the wider community legitimises empowerment and capacity building to help the community develop confidence and capability.	Distinctive contribution—individuals or groups bring particular contributions to the table on the basis of pooled responsibility and resources. Principled-localism—neighbourhood solutions within shared vision and principles (e.g., early years cooperatives, local sourcing, use of community space).
Connectedness and sense of place: Understanding the close interaction among economic, social, and environmental aspects within a locale. Shared experiences and appreciating what is distinctive and special about the local area, including landscape, biodiversity, architecture, and heritage. Cultural traditions in the area are also important in giving and defining an area's character.	Empathy and understanding of others' needs and aspirations, limitations. Coherence of identity (overlapping social and economic interactions). Strengthening and promotion of local identity through mutuality and reciprocity. Using local schools, shops, working near-to-home, mutually supportive neighbours, street markets, shared housing ownership schemes.
Intracommunity equity is the principle of equity between and within different communities and groups. It implies that consumption and production in one community should not undermine the ecological, social, and economic basis for other communities to maintain or improve their quality of life.	Providing affordable housing, diversity of employment, flexible and inclusive service design that meets the needs of all consumers, regardless of their abilities. Reinforcing health and individual and community wellbeing.

(*Continued*)

TABLE 8.1 (*Continued*)

Intergenerational equity is the principle of equity between people alive today and future generations. Unsustainable production and consumption by today's society could degrade the ecological, social, and economic basis for tomorrow's society, whereas community sustainability involves ensuring that future generations will have the means to achieve a quality of life equal to or better than today's.	Planning for the long-term vision, not just short-term gain or fix. Environmental stewardship schemes. Use of renewable energy; land and building reuse. Designing homes and spaces for lifetime needs, reducing the need to move. Co-housing—intergenerational, young and old mutually supporting each other.
Prosperous, resilient, and adaptable: Communities are capable of creating wealth and bouncing back from adverse situations and responding to the changing circumstances. Not only protecting against risks but also making/seeking opportunities. Investing in social capital, knowhow, and skills that are shared within and across neighbourhoods.	Cooperative investment, diverse training, premium support for skills and job opportunities. For those unable to gain paid work, being meaningfully engaged in neighbourhood. Capability and competence audits. Collective values are shared through community education and empowerment.
Shared external relationships: Open to outside ideas, people, and contributions.	Care for connected communities. Play a part in wider community as leader or beacon.

DEVELOPMENT MATRIX

We can translate these principles into a development matrix to show how compliance can progress a firm in general terms from initial engagement in community-focused thinking to embedded and adjusted products and services. The approach is similar to that in Chapter 7. (See Table 8.2.)

The questions compliance should be asking and this matrix is trying to map are:

- How can financial services contribute to wider community development?
- What exactly is its role as part of the community?

TABLE 8.2 Development matrix summary.

Outcome Principles	Start-up	Gaining Momentum	Embedding	Leadership and Innovation
Mutuality	■ Understanding strength of shared experiences and memories—start local newsletter, social group, or event.	■ Developing mixed energy sources in a policy that is owned by neighbourhood. ■ Increasing diversity of job opportunities.	■ Building *common vision*. ■ Mechanisms of cooperative working. ■ Ongoing community engagement.	■ Vision-led localised decision-making structures. ■ Deregulation in key areas. ■ Growing community capacity in local democracy and investment.
Engagement	■ Informal and formal. ■ Communications open to all interested parties (e.g., community meetings and newsletters).	■ Structured engagement programme is risk based. ■ Focus on responsiveness and cost-based reporting.	■ Systems of wider evaluation of sustainability (e.g., community health and happiness).	■ Engaging in national and international projects on sustainability. ■ Relationships that will help capacity building and peer-review roles (e.g., BS8904).

(Continued)

TABLE 8.2 (*Continued*)

Outcome Principles	Start-up	Gaining Momentum	Embedding	Leadership and Innovation
Intracommunity equity	■ Needs mapping, housing audits. ■ Skills development.	■ Shared identification of priorities (e.g., shared childcare, work–school partnerships, transport).	■ Working across communities with explicit aims to reduce disequilibria and enhance community contact and cooperation.	■ Celebrating cross-community collaboration beyond fixed-term projects; locally to internationally.
Prosperity	■ Responding to funding opportunities. ■ Standalone, "iconic" projects.	■ Immediate education, employment, and housing needs are demand-led.	■ Shared action/bidding for funds and marketing. ■ Creating new infrastructure for growth and reform. ■ Developing competitive edge for inward investment.	■ Cooperative promotion for inward investment. ■ Leadership nationally. ■ International coordinated promotion.

- What strategic actions such as the launch of certain products or new services would benefit the community principles listed previously and strengthen community resilience?
- What financial services actions should be avoided or deemphasised as they may undermine sustainable community development?

These broader perspectives give a more rounded picture of outcome that informs both regulators' views of their aims and also of individual financial services firms. These are only general examples and more detail can be produced for an individual firm.

CORPORATE SOCIAL RESPONSIBILITY

This focus on community outcome is not the same as corporate social responsibility (CSR). CSR is a framework for helping firms interact with community (usually defined as a wide range of stakeholders) in a responsible way. This is very valuable and worthwhile but is not the same as seeing the firm as part of the community without distinction between the two. This distinction can set up a rather awkward and stilted interplay, which is instinctively artificial and therefore hard to sustain, embed, and value.

CSR as a framework can become misdirected as a substitute for credible and effective community role. The philanthropy that is sometimes engendered (and by no means should be discouraged) is not a replacement for putting community at the heart of the business and understanding the wider needs we are all interested in, which may not be accurately of satisfactorily summarized by "rights" or "obligations" or CSR programmes.

CSR stakeholder engagement with outside partners, stakeholders, and the wider community is often seen as a bureaucratic or expensive add-on and not a driver of authenticity and well-rounded, values-led business. CSR engagement carried out thoroughly and genuinely is expensive and potentially high risk if the firm over-claims and is found wanting and is no substitute for a consumer outcomes approach.

NEW REPORTING STANDARDS

Community focus requires new forms of reporting. These are on the way. Some models listed in what follows are available now as templates, and others are in development. Many of these proprietary systems are partial and therefore incomplete. There is an undoubted need for integration and this is where financial and national standards bodies become essential. Perhaps most significant in the long term could be *integrated reporting*, a scheme published globally and in the UK in December 2013 and now being piloted by many leading corporations in a range of jurisdictions.

There are other new models emerging to help companies deal with such a community-focused approach. These include:

- AA1000SE—a framework for stakeholder engagement
- BS8900—developing and certifying sustainable systems
- Ethics mark—for ethics and values-led organisations and demonstrating authenticity
- BS8904/ISO 37101—setting a standard for sustainable and resilient communities
- ISO 26000—the international framework for CSR issues
- GRI (Global Reporting Initiative)—UN-sponsored reporting of sustainability
- Dow Jones Sustainability Index/FTSE4Good—indices of sustainability for listed companies
- Integrated reporting (IR)—evaluating the flows of value through business to community

BEHAVIOURAL ECONOMICS

Regulators are increasingly looking at community in a different way, trying to understand how behavioural psychology can help explain individual and collective decision making. This insight would allow firms to target their customers more effectively and help improve suitability.

Just one case is considered here in relation to those vulnerable customers who are in debt and looking for debt management solutions.

Seven Principles of Behavioural Economics:

1. *Other people's behaviour matters:* People do many things by observing others and copying; people are encouraged to continue to do things when they feel other people approve of their behaviour.
2. *Habits are important:* People do many things without consciously thinking about them. These habits are hard to change—even though people might want to change their behaviour, it is not easy for them.
3. *People are motivated to do the right thing:* There are cases where money is demotivating as it undermines people's intrinsic motivation.
4. *People's self-expectations influence how they behave:* They want their actions to be in line with their values and their commitments.
5. *People are loss-averse* and hang onto what they consider "theirs."
6. *People are bad at computation when making decisions:* They put undue weight on recent events and too little on far-off ones.

7. *People need to feel involved and effective to make a change:* Just giving people the incentives and information is not necessarily enough.

This behavioural approach is now informing regulatory policy development as seen in the recent FCA report on the annuities market. This connects with practical implementation of behavioural approaches 'on the ground' with firms using this to inform their product design and systems–such as the example from the newly-regulated sector debt management as shown in Figure 8.1. Example extracts of the regulatory approach from the report include:

> Competition in the [annuities] market is not working well for consumers. Many consumers are missing out by not shopping around for an annuity and switching providers, and some do not purchase the best annuity for their circumstances. Consumers' tendency to buy products from their existing provider weakens competitive pressure on incumbent firms and makes it harder for challenger firms to attract a critical mass of customers.
>
> From April 2015, in what is the biggest reform of the retirement system in a generation, [UK] consumers will be given much greater freedom over how to generate a retirement income from their pension savings. The reforms open up a range of choices, especially for those savers with smaller pension pots and those with other sources of retirement income.
>
> ... pension savers display well-known biases, such as a tendency to underestimate longevity, inflation and investment risk. We also found that the choices savers make are highly sensitive to how the options are presented (framing effects), which means that consumers may make different decisions, even when the underlying choice remains the same, depending on the way the information is provided.
>
> However, there is a risk that greater choice and more complex products will reduce consumers' confidence and appetite to shop around ... behavioral factors noted above make savers vulnerable to being sold products which do not best meet their needs.[4]

FCA Proposals:

- Require firms to make it clear to consumers how their quote compares relative to other providers' on the open market.
- Options should be presented in a way that supports good decision making rather than driving sales of particular products ... consideration should be given to appropriate framing, including use of behavioural triggers such as a rule of thumb to use when withdrawing funds.
- Reforming *wake-up packs* designed to prompt holders to reconsider theory options.
- Development of a "pensions dashboard" that would enable consumers to view all their lifetime pension savings (including their state pension) in one place.

Other people's behaviour matters: People do many things by observing others and copying; people are encouraged to continue to do things when they feel other people approve of their behaviour.

Habits are important: People do many things without consciously thinking about them. These habits are hard to change—even though people might want to change their behaviour, it is not easy for them.

People are motivated to "do the right thing": There are cases where money is demotivating as it undermines people's intrinsic motivation.

People's self-expectations influence how they behave: They want their actions to be in line with their values and their commitments.

People are loss-averse and hang on to what they consider theirs.

People are bad at computation when making decisions: They put undue weight on recent events and too little on far-off ones.

People need to feel involved and effective to make a change: Just giving people the incentives and information is not necessarily enough.

Debt Map—Individuals can see a real indication of peer debt activity within their postcode through an online tool.
Living Room—Web portal allows consumers to share their experience and develop a sense of community.
Case Studies—Showcasing individual experiences with debt through case studies featured on the Living Room. It gives other consumers the confidence to comment, relate, and share their experiences.

Planfinder/Self-help Pack—developed tools with the input of our customers to allow them to review their finances and easily understand what financial habits they would like to change.

Live Again—Practical debt solutions to help a client not only manage their debts, but also to live their lives.

Segmentation and profiling of our customers has allowed us to understand more about their values. Pen portraits of these.

Solutions—Entering into a debt plan for what could be a short amount of time gives the client the opportunity to keep what is theirs (their house, car, etc.).

Annual reviews help the client plan and prepare for the future by giving them the tools to budget each month for events that might happen in the future, therefore helping minimise any worry.

Initial call—The client is given all the options available to them from their very first call. They are encouraged to make a decision as to which one is the most effective for them. The clients are in control of every decision throughout their debt plan.
Self-Help Pack—Developed tools with the input of our customers to allow them to review and take control of their finances themselves.

FIGURE 8.1 Seven Principles of Behavioural Economics. By Permission Pay Plan Ltd

This is a key determinant of community outcome as millions have pension provisions affected by these products and the recently announced liberalization of the market. How individuals respond will shape the overall wealth and health of, particularly, aging communities. This is an area that will receive a great deal of attention internationally and will place a new raft of requirements on firms that compliance will need to understand, interpret, and apply. The reputational stakes are high.

VULNERABLE CONSUMERS

One area where regulation and compliance is developing a direct interest in community is in trying to address the needs of vulnerable sections of the community—a concern that is as much founded on an intention to improve the overall financial and wider health of the community or society as it is about mitigating the risk of poor outcomes for individual consumers.

This macro-outcome view is a perspective on collective outcomes and recognises that to some extent the outcomes that are achieved by individuals are dependent on the outcomes achieved by others around them. An analysis of collective outcomes also builds upon the work of behavioural economics. This scaling up of outcome is mediated by firms and producers that will provide services and products partly based on how the collection of "others" behave.

Intervention by regulators must conventionally be on the basis of market failure but in this case the driving principles are really the purposes of community described earlier, including the principles of inter- and intra-generational equity. These are so politically and socially sensitive that they provide an override in policy development and compliance practice. One area where this focus is emerging is in relation to consumer credit (a sector newly regulated by FCA), which touches upon collective debt levels and the care firms need to take of vulnerable consumers. But what is vulnerable and what should compliance focus on?

We look here at the case of vulnerable consumers in relation to FCA's interest in consumer credit using extracts from the key FCA report.

Summary of FCA's Consumer Credit and Consumers in Vulnerable Circumstances Report (April 2014)[5]   This report sets out categories of vulnerable consumers, the factors that affect vulnerability, and some of the coping strategies used, particularly in relation to consumer credit.

Further research on vulnerable consumers was published by FCA in February 2015, informing ongoing development of the regulatory regime in this sector.

Definition of "Consumers in Vulnerable Circumstances":
Vulnerability is such a subjective term that it is hard to define. Indeed, most users of consumer credit may be regarded as "vulnerable" to some degree because of their financial circumstance. [FCA] considers a vulnerable consumer to be someone who, due to their personal circumstances, is *especially susceptible to detriment* ...
... detriment can manifest itself in many ways. For example:

People can choose the wrong product;

pay a high price;

fail to get the right product that serves their needs; and

be treated unfairly by their chosen provider.

However, the most significant detriment occurs when people, through the use of consumer credit, get into unmanageable or problem debt. This can often lead to spiralling problems, leading to both financial and nonfinancial costs.

There are three distinct borrower groups:

1. Survival borrowers, due to very tight finances, often feel they have no option but to borrow due to lack of income. Catalogue credit and home credit are very popular forms of credit with this group due to ease of access and low weekly payments.
2. Lifestyle borrowers also use catalogue and home credit, but for different reasons. These borrowers generally have sufficient income for day-to-day expenses but use credit for larger purchases or one-off events, and feel in control when minimum payments are being met. Debts can become unmanageable, and the strategies people use to cope with spiralling debts show how unmanageable debt triggers both financial detriment and affects health and wellbeing.
3. Reluctant borrowers, who tend to limit their use of credit, focus on paying back existing debts, often from more mainstream sources such as bank loans and credit cards.

There is extensive evidence showing that people are particularly susceptible to detriment when they:

- Experience changes in their circumstances (e.g., change of income, interest rate changes, illness, separation, family loss)
- Have built up high levels of accumulated debt with high repayment ratios

Vulnerability can be related to individual factors such as:

- Financial literacy
- Levels of confidence
- Character and self-control or determination

Vulnerable consumers are often those with … low income and lack of savings … often younger adults, those in receipt of [welfare] benefits and those living in rented accommodation. Vulnerable consumers may also be those with mental health problems, the elderly and those who live alone.

Coping strategies include:

- Cutting out nonessentials (although for some this may mean choosing between food and heating)
- Making only minimum payments
- Juggling between creditors
- Skipping payments short term
- Borrowing from family and friends
- Ignoring contacts from creditors
- Seeking external advice and debt management

Vulnerable consumers are heavily influenced by flexibility, control, and familiarity over absolute cost:

- *Flexibility:* Users prefer flexible repayments and prefer to use lenders that recognise the difficultly of maintaining regular payments and allow people to be let off missed payments. Aligned to this is the importance of control and the feeling that more traditional lenders gave little control around what people could borrow and no bargaining power to influence the terms and conditions.
- *Certainty of approval and repayments:* Those on low incomes wanted to be certain that they would get the money they needed before they applied. Many did not use banks and credit cards due to fear of rejection. While some had experiences in the past of being turned down by providers, for some this was a perception of what would happen if they applied for mainstream credit.
- *Familiarity and trust:* People lacked familiarity with some forms of lending and were more likely to use lenders that they (and often their friends and family) had previously used. This preference for familiarity is also shown in being receptive to face-to-face contact from lenders, valuing personal service, and often seeing mainstream lenders as remote and impersonal.

The objective of regulation and compliance is to find strategies that help to identify consumers who may be vulnerable, steer them away from poor outcomes, or mitigate poor outcomes when they arise. The key is preventing or reducing the circumstances that may contribute to vulnerability. In this sense it is very much part of the prevention agenda but draws upon outcome measures for its direction that in turn are justified in terms of overall community health as much as individual consumer detriment.

CONCLUSION

What we connect to in terms of family, places, value, brands, organisations, and communities determines how we see desirable outcomes. It is not enough for compliance to measure outcome purely in financial terms. Consumers may well be looking for other outcomes and prioritise these above or alongside financial return and security. Wider society will also be looking for banks and financial sectors to be delivering outcomes in terms of enterprise culture, investment, environmental security, and many other factors. These are the real tests, the ultimate arbiters of compliance performance, not obeying process rules. A lack of breaches is increasingly not enough, and community will emerge as the primary driver of compliance in the years to come so that it may justify a separate stage 6.

ENDNOTES

1. Adair Turner, chairman, FSA, speech at the City Banquet (London: The Mansion House, Sept. 22, 2009).
2. David Jackman, ISO 37101 (Sustainable Development of Communities consultation 2015).
3. Adapted from BS8904, *Developing Sustainable Communities*, by chair and author, David Jackman (2011).
4. FCA, MS14/3.2, *Retirement Income Market Study: Interim Report* (Nov. 12, 2014).
5. http://www.fca.org.uk/static/documents/research-papers/consumer-credit-customers-vulnerable-circumstances.pdf.

CHAPTER 9

Corporate Faith

I was thinking about the rubbish, the flapping plastic in the branches, the shore-line of odd stuff caught along the fencing, and I half-closed my eyes and imagined this was the spot where everything I'd ever lost since my childhood had washed up, and I was now standing here in front of it, and if I waited long enough, a tiny figure would appear on the horizon across the field, and gradually get larger until ...

—Kazuo Ishiguro, *Never Let Me Go* (London: Faber and Faber, 2005), 282

Corporate faith may seem an unusual expression but it directs us to a set of connecting forces and a repository of commitment that is fundamental. *Faith* here is not meant in a religious sense but rather is intended to encapsulate all that is central to corporate ethics, culture, governance, and outcomes (including community). In other words, corporate faith synthesises all that we have considered so far, operating as an overarching layer that makes sense of all that has gone before and offers an exciting approach that draws these threads together and affects them in a deeper, coordinated, and more effective way. This is the missing link and the key to success in compliance.

All the elements discussed so far—ethics, culture, governance, outcomes, and community—may seem rather disconnected. They are linked in a sequential sense where one seems naturally to lead to the need for and development of the next in a series of layers as seen in Figure 9.1. In this chapter we consider the deeper sinews that connect them and in the final chapter we draw out what has been implicit throughout, the process that drives development from stage to stage, from element to element, and ultimately, from an *evolution* to a *revolution* of maturity.

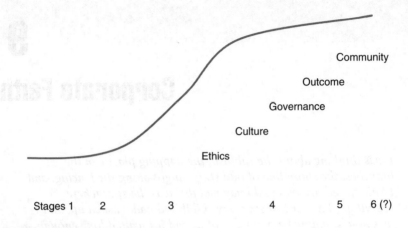

FIGURE 9.1 Elements of Maturity

WHAT IS CORPORATE FAITH?

Corporations, companies, and organisations are more than collections of individuals; they are communities in themselves that have the following fundamentals:

- Purpose, role, identity, and responsibilities
- Assumptions and beliefs
- Power and structures
- Aspirations and views of the future
- Values and commitment

Taken together, this amounts to *corporate faith*, and it is these underlying factors, at board level and throughout the organisation, that shape:

- Strategy
- Decision making
- Values, ethics, and attitudes
- Culture: ways of operating and systemic practises
- Behaviour
- Relationships internally and externally
- Reputation and trustworthiness
- Attitudes towards risk
- Ultimately, long- and short-term performance

In other words, corporate faith underpins and informs the major threads we have highlighted here and that have been the successive focus of regulation and compliance: ethics, culture, governance, and outcome.

It is sometimes the case that this storage of corporate faith in the firm's processes and practices can become a drag on its evolution, responsiveness, and positive development. This *lag effect* is a form of *compliance risk*, and a contributor to other risks when aggregated with them. Corporate faith needs to be open, responsive, and continually evolving to absorb and deal with new environmental conditions, changing market conditions, competitor pressure and consumer expectations and, critically, emerging regulatory requirements. As with the revolution in regulatory approaches described in earlier chapters, corporate faith becomes the main way of transmitting change and ensuring it is embedded and sustainable.

MANAGING CORPORATE FAITH

To understand and better direct and manage corporate faith allows the business—and regulation and compliance—to become more coherent, connected, and effective. It is the key access point to enable compliance to enter the very heart and workings of the business, to make all other aspects align and commit and behave consistently in a compliant, values-led way. Quite simply, it is the key to success but also contains the seeds of disaster.

The addressing and manipulation of corporate faith is very sophisticated and requires precise microsurgery. Indeed, the very concept of manipulating faith might sound inappropriate. That is correct. Here the attitude, intent, values, and ethics used in enabling change are as crucial to success as the operation of developing corporate faith itself. Cynical manipulation simply will not work.

Businesses often use *mission statements* and talk of rebuilding trust, brand values, corporate responsibility, social engagement, and working by the spirit and not the letter of the rules. This "spirituality" may have no religious connection but the principles of working with and among deeper issues of ethics, commitment, and community remain profoundly the same.

THE VALUE OF CORPORATE FAITH

A focus on corporate faith is valuable because:

1. Corporate faith deals with fundamental causes that affect the entire corporate character and operation. To influence corporate faith is the most cost-effective lever for change. Interventions further down the decision-making chain may need to be more substantial and becomes difficult to embed.

2. The dimensions of corporate faith are immediately understandable and commonplace in businesses and organisations of all types; they connect with the everyday experiences, priorities, and issues of customers, staff, the media, shareholders, and increasingly, regulators.
3. Corporate faith directly relates through corporate ethics and culture to conduct risk and consumer outcome—areas of regulatory focus.
4. Corporate faith unites intention to action; it provides a rationale for values, standards, decisions, and measurement; it offers answers to the question, "Why?"
5. An analysis of corporate faith directly addresses the shared assumptions that have frequently underpinned systemic failures, including the 2008 financial crisis.
6. Corporate faith is cross-cultural and evolutionary; it is principles based, allowing for the flexible interpretation and implementation of principles and practices.
7. Community engagement and sustainability in corporate faith are key to securing positive outcomes.

We identify five dimensions:

1. Purpose, role, identity, and responsibilities
2. Beliefs and assumptions
3. Power and structures
4. Aspirations and views of the future
5. Individual responsibility, values, and commitment

Each represents a bundle of questions that we insist are translated into real business applications. The programme's aim is to connect deeper sinews of corporate life with practical outcomes and commercial benefits. A compelling business case could be made, but a business case is not always the only or the best starting point. We believe a focus on corporate faith assists businesses and organisations of any size or sector to:

- Enhance performance.
- Deliver effective change.
- Create a marketing edge.
- Attract quality, committed employees.
- Enhance reputation, trust, and authenticity.
- Build regulatory relationships.

DIMENSIONS OF CORPORATE FAITH

Here are some ideas of what might be covered under the five dimensions. Many of these connect with themes discussed in earlier chapters, taking them to a deeper level of significance and closer connectivity.

Dimension 1: Purpose, Role, Identity, and Responsibilities

The board may want to start with considering the company's purpose and could start by asking the following questions:

- Why do you do what you do?
- What drives your actions and plans?
- What are you trying to achieve?
- What is the purpose of your organisation?
- What is the wider impact of what you do?
- Why is it worthwhile?
- What really drives your organisation?

The purpose of companies is a complex subject and depends upon the concept of community discussed in Chapter 8.

Dimension 2: Beliefs and Assumptions

Businesses and sectors work on basic shared assumptions, such as:

- Acceptable rates of pay and bonuses
- Normal levels of service and their costs and conditions
- Behaviour towards customers
- Educational entry requirements and qualifications
- Supposed value to customers, communities, and society
- Levels of acceptable risk

These assumptions will be embedded in company practice, the experiences of staff, the prejudices of board members, presentational messages to government and shareholders, pay rates, university and college course curricula, and in statements in the press. These assumptions are often deeply ingrained and rarely challenged. Challenge is resisted where it occurs with superficial argument. For example, when the levels of bonuses in financial services were challenged post-2008, the common response of firms and industry bodies was that without bonuses it would be impossible to attract suitably skilled bankers. Assumptions usually can be changed slowly. It was not so long ago that bankers were paid percentages of their salary as bonuses; somehow this became multiples in the 1990s, and so it is not impossible for bonuses once again to become percentages, if only 100 percent.

Assumptions also exist in how customers can be treated. This is one of the targets of the TCF initiative, which aims to alter the fundamental relationship between firm benefit and customer benefit. Similarly, the UK's Retail Distribution Review addresses what seemed to be an unstoppable transition from commission selling to fee-based advice. The assumption that commission was the only way to find suitable advice for the majority has been challenged, but it has created the difficulty that many cannot or will not pay fees. The education task is not just in changing the assumptions in the industry but also changing the perceptions of consumers. Identifying in-built, unchallenged assumptions can be the job of NEDs, particularly those brought in from other sectors who may see afresh and view the basics very differently. Beliefs may be even more entrenched and will include trust in certain market trends, for example, the belief in 2007–2008 that house prices would continue to rise and never fall, which proved to be a very faulty view. Belief might also be in technologies or tools such as risk management.

Dimension 3: Power and Structures

The balance of power in financial services has long been characterised by the advantageous position of capital over worker, buyer over seller, and the firm over its customers. The latter is typically seen as being underpinned by the disequilibrium of information and understanding between financial services professionals and unsophisticated customers who just want an easy explanation and a quick fix. But the location of power fundamental to the working of financial services is much more complicated than that and is shifting.

Power is distributed within structures, maintained by processes, and hedged by regulations. But as time has progressed the structures have changed; banks have become larger, globalised, multifunction corporations with little allegiance to any one product, country, or market. They have in some sense risen above the cords of control that have sought to bind them. On the other hand, consumers have become in general more educated and demanding and have organised themselves into pressure groups that lobby industry and government. Consumers represent votes in modern liberal democracies. Banks and other institutions cannot escape collective public will that is also internationalising and taking form through global regulatory bodies and coordinated strategies, for example, the Foreign Account Tax Compliance Act (FATCA).

Ring-Fencing In the UK, Sir John Vickers and the Independent Commission on Banking (ICB) provided recommendations for creating a stronger and more competitive banking sector without exposing taxpayers to the costs of those banks failing in a disorderly manner.

Ring-fencing prohibits banks that accept retail deposits from undertaking a range of activities that are not directly connected to providing payment services and making loans. The "Volcker Rule"—in the process of being implemented in the United States—does something similar, but is less restrictive. Its focus is on constraining the ability of banks to undertake proprietary trading.

However, ring-fencing delivers additional benefits compared with the Volcker Rule. Most of a bank's global wholesale and investment banking operations, and the risks they entail, would be separated from everyday retail banking. This—and limits on the extent to which a ring-fenced bank can deal with other entities in its wider banking group and other financial institutions—insulates the ring-fenced bank and makes it more resolvable in the event it runs into trouble.

Dimension 4: Aspirations and Views of the Future

Industries or firms may have in-built views of the future, both positive and negative. They may base a good deal of their decision making on these views. Risk appetite relates closely to these views of the future and they may be highly misplaced.

It is, of course, very difficult to see the future. But compliance departments must have as part of their basic working practices the function of *horizon scanning*. This is not just scanning for compliance risks, which so often translate into forthcoming regulatory changes, but for anything that may alter the landscape in terms of the five threads highlighted in this text, such as emerging views on ethics, unexpected influences on corporate culture, governance changes internally or across the sector, new measures of outcome, or tectonic shifts in basic assumptions.

The basic economic environment sets the framework for all compliance work, it dictates the pressure on resources and the temptations to mis-sell to meet targets, it affects incentives and creates uncertainty. Right now there is a great deal of economic uncertainty: Will austerity in western, developed countries restore prosperity or slide into deflation and stagnation? Will the Eurozone suffer as the United States, and possibly even the UK, accelerates and start to raise interest rates? Will China and other ASEAN nations keep up their current pace or suffer from internal pressures reminiscent of 2008, or will India emerge just in time and ride to the rescue? What about the resource-rich nations of Africa and South America? These will all emerge in good time, but it is necessary for compliance to have a view because the general economic situation affects how cultures operate and firms view risk.

Similarly, there is a need for compliance to have a view of regulatory change. This is not only with reference to your own sector and jurisdiction, but internationally and across sectors. What happens today in a different sector and a far-off jurisdiction can travel quickly and also influence local decisions by providing precedents and new points for triangulation.

Dimension 5: Values

This dimension develops our thinking on ethics in Chapter 4 and culture in Chapter 5. Values are slightly different from ethics in that they may not be necessarily good in a universal ethical sense but they will be "goods" from your firm's perspective. What your firm values or prioritises may include shareholder return, customer service, and profit. These may have some ethical elements within them, but they are not *pure* ethics and others may take issue with the way these values are applied or the results they achieve. Values are designed for action rather than providing an ideological framework.

Firms use value statements to express their mission or style or just the ways they want to be seen as being different. They are unlike codes as they have less of the normative flavour about them and are more an assertion of worth.

EXAMPLE: RBS

Our Values

Serving Customers:
- We exist to serve customers.
- We earn their trust by focusing on their needs and delivering excellent service.

Working Together:
- We care for each other and work best as one team.
- We bring the best of ourselves to work and support one another to realise our potential.

Doing the Right Thing:

- We do the right thing.

- We take risk seriously and manage it prudently.

- We prize fairness and inclusion and exercise judgment with thought and integrity.

Thinking Long Term:

- We know we succeed only when our customers and communities succeed.

- We do business in an open, direct, and sustainable way.

HOW FAITH DEVELOPS

Building corporate faith is essentially an internal learning process. Corporate faith holds the collective memory of compliance and regulation and it is constantly being reconsidered and interpreted differently. Similarly, we can speak about the *regulatory faith*, that is, the underlying assumptions and cumulative learning held in and about the regulatory-compliance system. In reality, the General Model should not be shown as a smooth curve but more of a spiral of learning with a circular motion that revisits and reimagines earlier elements. (See Figure 9.2.)

To regard regulation as cyclical is a cynical misunderstanding and one of the strengths of a mature regulatory-compliance system is to value reinterpretations and to learn from setbacks rather than being easily blown off course or becoming self-indulgent.

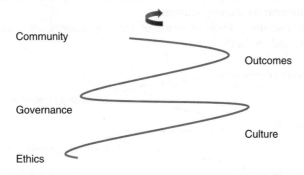

FIGURE 9.2 Spiral of Learning in Interrelation of Elements of Corporate Faith

CORPORATE FAITH INTO PRACTICE

Corporate faith develops in compliance and regulation through practice. The five elements described in Chapters 4–8 are all active. You practice ethics, live and mould culture, govern, generate outcomes, live faith, and 'commune'. They are not states to be achieved, a virtue to be recognized and accredited, or a standard that once reached is forgotten. Here is a constant struggle, a muddle sometimes, a trying out, a set of questions, and partial answers—always a journey, never a conclusion. Compliance, like much else, is destined to be always an activity, a practice. In line with other professions, compliance is a *craft*, not an academic pursuit. This requires a realization that each element here must be lived and practiced if they are to work. If you rewrite each element as an activity, the whole process becomes more useful, real, and effective. Forging forward, often in the dark, learning from experience, testing, creating new approaches, twisting these threads again, and maybe adding new ones is the essential lesson of this book. And that is the excitement and the challenge. (See Figure 9.3.)

PROFESSIONALISM

Competence can be viewed as a minimum standard. Regulators are increasingly emphasizing the need for expertise in certain roles and are looking for a demonstration that employees can operate in new and unfamiliar situations.

Professionalism is a more advanced concept than competence. It involves:

- High levels of knowledge, skill, and application
- Proven ability to see the whole picture and not just a narrow specialism
- Commitment to integrity and professional values and conduct
- Commitment to lifelong learning
- Giving something back in terms of training colleagues, advancing the subject, and so forth

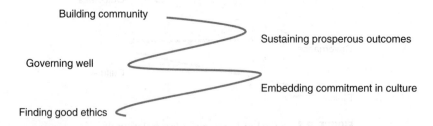

FIGURE 9.3 Active Compliance Landscape

Professionalism is often conferred and protected by a professional body such as the ICA—the International Compliance Association. This serves the purpose of controlling entry standards and has the right to censure or remove individuals who do not maintain these standards. It also provides services to the profession and is a channel by which individual professionals can give back to the body of the profession (e.g., as examiners).

Compliance *professionals* deserve a higher status in society and in business and usually are remunerated accordingly. They are often the go-to people for advice and guidance for subject matters that include careers and education. If compliance can step up, then it is an established and recognized profession internationally.

How Compliance Develops

This is a new and exciting prospectus for compliance and places the function on a sounder and higher-status footing. Up until this point we have studiously avoided referring to compliance practitioners as professional. After this point, we do consider it is reasonable to regard compliance as a *profession* and practitioners as *professionals*.

Why is this? By this stage in the general development model compliance as a function has taken on a wider range of new methodologies, roles and responsibilities resulting in a significant increase in the degree of sophistication involved. This requires a higher level of skill and especially more complex judgment and this is a key to practicing a profession. Also the previous chapters have placed a greater emphasis on ethics, integrity, and individual standards, and it would not be possible to operate in these areas if practitioners did not take on a level of professional integrity.

Therefore, beyond stage 5 it is possible to say that a profession has fully emerged with more advanced ways of working. Professionalization has implications for salary, recruitment, and internal status as well as external recognition. This step also increases the need for formal qualifications, registration with a professional body, full disclosure, a professional code and disciplinary processes, and proper professional development. The ICA (International Compliance Association) provides such opportunities and a clear professional route. In 2015, it issued its new Ethics Code (prepared by the author) which appears in Chapter 4. Compliance officers should be on the board with this general direction of travel if they wish to progress both individually and as a profession.

All that we have discussed in this and in previous chapters suggests that compliance is a serious, strategic, and high-level function that can add significant value to the business. Compliance must step up and accept the considerable challenges in this book and learn new techniques and approaches. This partly involves more compliance education.

New areas for compliance to develop competence are:

- Horizon-scanning
- Identifying and analyzing new nonstandard (non-rulebook) points of reference
- Creating environments conducive to ethics, constructive challenge, and pro-compliance culture
- Developing a strategic role
- Engaging skillfully and valuably in constructive challenge
- Understanding the business better
- Having a point of view
- Making judgments beyond yes/no
- Reflecting to the business community needs/expectations
- Understanding and foreseeing changing regulatory expectations
- Analyzing and calibrating outcome
- Assuring community outcomes
- Facilitating internal and external education

JUDGMENT-BASED COMPLIANCE

Compliance needs to learn to deal with *depth* as well as complexity. It is clear that all the threads teased out here—ethics, culture, governance, outcomes, and community—may have risen, or are now rising, to prominence sequentially but they are interconnected and should be seen and addressed as a whole. They represent a deep, sensitive, responsible, professional approach to important issues that lie squarely in the lap of financial services and many other industries. These issues should never be brushed aside with some terribly simplistic, mechanical tick-box tool, but deserve full and weighted consideration. Judgment lies at the heart of getting this right, of stepping up, and it is judgment that should be rewarded.

CONCLUSION

This brief chapter moves compliance into a fundamentally different level with deeper concerns and an attention to the common threads that bind the firm's compliance activities together, and provides the foundation for change and professional standing.

CHAPTER 10

Corporate Maturity

*But the horses didn't want it—they swerved apart; the earth didn't
want it, sending up rocks through which riders must pass single
file; the temples, the tank, the jail, the palace, the birds, the carrion,
the Guest House, that came into view as they issued from the gap
and saw Mau beneath: they didn't want it, they said in their
hundred voices, "No, not yet," and the sky said, "No, not there."*
—E. M. Forster, *A Passage to India* (London:
Penguin, 1924), 316

This final chapter sets out the direction of travel and processes of change.
The essential question for compliance is *how to ensure change is effective and embedded*. The answer comes from understanding the processes
underlying change.

Corporate maturity is a framework for recognising embeddedness and
explaining the processes that underpin continual, and sometimes revolutionary, change. It is an overall measure of compliance success.

WHAT IS MATURITY?

Maturity is a summative way of describing the quality of the internal compliance system of a firm or sector. It combines:

- sound ethics,
- embedded in corporate culture and conduct,
- led and overseen by good governance,
- towards positive consumer outcomes, and
- contributing to sustainable and resilient communities.

Maturity has a number of important values to regulation and compliance as the concept provides:

- A measure of overall compliance performance
- A direction of travel for all compliance activity
- An understanding of the key processes of change

Maturity is an overall measure of compliance health that a regulator can use to determine the level of regulatory risk a firm poses and to determine appropriate types of intervention and relationship, while compliance professionals can use maturity as a measure of their own success. If regulators can measure maturity successfully and reliably, it is possible to use this to determine whether a firm should be dealt with in a proactive and interventionist fashion or more as a responsible partner. In short, it is possible to say whether a firm acts in a childlike way (responding only to being told what to do) or as an adult (foreseeing and avoiding problems for itself with minimal oversight). We can all imagine a naughty child in the back of the class being dealt with in a completely different way from the well-motivated (and successful) mature student. Regulators and compliance can then tailor their interventions to improving that level of maturity.

The following schema describes five stages of development of corporate maturity for a single firm but this sequence can also be applied to a sector or an industry as a whole. The stages are not watertight or mutually exclusive, but show a general set of characteristics that may be true of a group or part of a group. They are typified by *attitudes* to regulation and compliance and the questions compliance is most typically asked. These range from "Tell me what I have to do to avoid getting caught" to "Have we ticked all the boxes?" to "Give me the business case" to "We'll do it right, anyway."

The level of compliance resource, reward, and status varies accordingly and as corporate maturity reflects the development of the compliance function as it becomes more strategic and judgment based. Developing maturity therefore provides a *direction of travel* for compliance planning and for regulators—and has implications in reducing both of their costs and rebalancing the range of compliance and regulatory techniques. The aim of this focus is to bring prevention and risk reduction ahead of reactive firefighting and remediation in a meaningful, substantive way.

Improvements in corporate maturity allow more advanced regulatory styles and methodologies, moving from police officer to educator to (almost) partner (*almost* because a regulator must always remain a regulator and retain a significant degree of independence and avoid regulatory capture at all costs).

This shift of regulatory relationship has enormous implications for the kinds of strategies regulators can deploy and how sophisticated they can risk becoming. The implications for firms are also considerable, delivering what is sometimes referred to as a *regulatory dividend* in terms of cost reduction and reducing bureaucracy. The maturity of firms and regulation working together delivers improved regulatory and community outcomes and this is self-reinforcing, through building of public trust and system-wide regulatory reputation.

This *maturity shift* is a parallel but interconnected journey between the regulators and the industry where the regulators and the industry develop maturity alongside and in support of each other. One cannot advance ahead of the other. If the regulator gets ahead of the industry and treats firms as mature that are not so, it could be severely caught out, appearing too "light-touch" (as happened in 2008). Conversely, if firms get ahead of themselves and develop mature compliance systems that the regulator cannot or will not recognize, especially at the supervisory interface, then the firms leave themselves open to the risk of fine or sanction. It is a delicate road to tread that requires a lot of close dialogue and the building of mutual understanding.

MATURITY AND A DIRECTION OF TRAVEL

The diagram in Table 10.1 offers an overall view of corporate and regulatory maturity and a direction of travel for regulation and compliance. There are five levels of corporate maturity.

> *Level 1—Noncompliance:* This is where a firm is unaware or unwilling to subject itself to any compliance activity, bar registration, in order to obtain the necessary license to practice.
>
> *Level 2—Minimum standards:* Here a firm could be just starting up or simply unsophisticated in its compliance operations, just doing as little as possible to get away with and not be caught. A firm may only have sufficient capital requirements and the basic threshold conditions. Some firms see this as a rational long-term position, keeping compliance costs to the minimum and taking on board any subsequent fines as an operational cost. These may be commonly regarded as serial offenders, and in this state they are difficult for regulators to deal with as they have insufficient traction, especially if the firm is operating internationally and is officially classified as too-big-to-fail.
>
> *Level 3—Compliance culture:* The firm is doing exactly what it is told to do by regulators in a mechanistic, tick-box way. This is the position of too many large firms that seem to feel comfortable with an

TABLE 10.1 Levels of corporate maturity.

Values and Culture of Firms	Compliance and Regulation
Noncompliance	
Minimum Standards	
■ Hopes never to be caught	■ Perimeter policing
■ As little as can be got away with	■ Basic licensing
■ Compliance an unwelcome cost	■ Early intervention—use of enforcement
■ Tries to abdicate decisions and responsibilities	■ Threshold conditions—de-authorization
	■ Rationalizing sector by raising standards—cannot meet requirements (e.g., capital)
Compliance Culture	
■ Unthinking, mechanical compliance—comfort blanket	■ Costly to regulate
■ By the book—black or white	■ Need to explain and check focus
■ "Tell me what I have to do"	■ Spin and reporting—obfuscation
■ Business prevention	■ Audit dependence
■ Bureaucracy costly	■ Governance responsibility narrow
■ Culture of dependency	
Business Improvement	
■ Risk focused, self-policing	■ Converging regulatory outcomes
■ Some buying in at senior level	■ Themed visits
■ Ethos integrated into most business processes	■ Risk reduced—reputational benefits
■ Seen as assisting business and reputation	
Values-Led	
■ Internalized core values at all levels	■ Partnership relationship
■ Outcome focused	■ Ethical culture embedded
■ Compliance by spirit, not letter	■ Sustainable regulation
■ Values focused, goes beyond rules, not just compliance	■ Robust risk control
■ Well-developed individual responsibility	■ Lower cost
■ Ethical Spaces and learning culture	■ Community aligned
■ Awareness and discussion of ethical considerations at all levels	■ Builds trust
	■ Consumer education and engagement

industrial-scale approach. This unimaginative situation appears to be the best way of minimizing risk and ensuring customer protection. It is also safe in relation to competitors, although it is often here that complacency can develop, allowing the emerging or largest risks never to be identified or spoken about (as in 2008). It is usually the most expensive overall and often the least cost-effective place to be. This is the position where the compliance question is more likely to be "Show me where it says we can't … " rather than "How can we improve our standards and conduct our business with integrity?"

Level 4—Business improvement: This means developing compliance on the basis of a business case, seeing compliance as a value and as contributing towards business goals. But in pressured situations the business needs/targets may well squeeze out such good intent. This can be a potentially fragile position that can backfire if the firm suffers a public compliance failure, as has happened frequently since 2008. The advantages of this position are summarized in Table 10.2.

Level 5—Values-led: This is doing the right thing because you *want* to. Compliance is internalized, based on self-determined values that drive how business is carried out throughout the organisation. A truly values-led culture is a culture that is supportive of the aims of compliance (i.e., the principles and values implicit in regulation are subsumed within by the firm's own values). This is a desirable position as it is effective and so offers a direction of travel for the compliance department.

It is level 5 that introduces the concept of unconditionality, developed in the next section.

This categorization highlights the difference in attitude that comes with and drives increased maturity and such a shift does not usually happen

TABLE 10.2 Business case for ethical culture versus ticking boxes.

Ethical Culture	Ticking Boxes
▪ Strengthens relationship with client and improves business ▪ Small print unnecessary—key information spelled out in plain English ▪ Balanced scorecard ▪ Regulatory dividend ▪ Customers behaving more responsibly and with greater understanding	▪ Clients inclined to switch firms ▪ Complaints slow ▪ Disclaimers on all communications ▪ Opportunity for confusion and mis-selling ▪ Reputational/regulatory loss ▪ Consumers more likely to dispute, feeling dissatisfied

Exercises

1. You may wish to try to classify your firm, or other firms you know well, under this categorization. Give reasons for your classification.
2. Now use the classification to map out a broad way forward for improving the maturity of your firm and to plan how you may progress compliance in the long term.
3. With whom should you share this model? Why? What response do you hope for?

---

overnight. Developing maturity usually takes some time and is difficult to rush, even if you have buy-in at the top of an organization. It is suggested that it is almost necessary to go through the pain of the failures of early levels and experience the basic difficulties before a more mature attitude and culture can emerge and become embedded. It is probably not possible to skip levels.

It is unrealistic to see progression between these levels as mechanical and crudely sequential. Various elements of all levels are operating at the same time. The realistic position is to establish how each theme mentioned in Table 10.1 can be worked together. It is also possible, even likely, that any firm slips back in times of stress or due to inevitable phases of complacency. It takes constant vigilance and compliance pressure to keep moving forward.

This model gives a unity to the whole of Chapters 4 to 8 and coherence to the criteria for judgment-based compliance explained in Chapter 9. It should therefore no longer be necessary for compliance to operate in the dark or purely pragmatically; here is a roadmap that offers a guide to the past, present, and most particularly for the future. It is now possible to frame a *compliance 10-year plan*, not just a 1-year programme that follows on from what was done the year before. The map in Table 10.1 now needs to be used by regulators and compliance together and consistently and internationally for the long term.

Maturity Stage by Stage

Maturity develops independently from the General Model of regulatory and compliance systems set out in Chapter 2. But the process that drives maturity deeper also drives the long-term progression from stage to stage along that development curve. To understand how this works we need to look more closely at the interrelationship between the stages and levels.

For example, as in Table 10.3, maturity can be tracked as regulation and compliance progress along the development curve and the proportion of firms in each level changes.

TABLE 10.3 Example of tracking development of corporate maturity.

	Stage 1	Stage 2	Stage 3	Stage 4	Stage 5
Level 1	30	20	5	5	0
Level 2	50	70	30	10	5
Level 3	10	5	50	40	30
Level 4	5	5	10	30	30
Level 5	5	0	5	15	35

Estimated percentages of firms in each maturity level at each stage of development in the General Model.

Table 10.3 Notes:

1. It seems perfectly possible that in the early stages of regulatory development there can be firms that excel to the highest level of maturity, although it will be in the context of a relatively simple compliance regime and some may fall back as the regime develops and becomes more sophisticated and demanding.
2. The dominant category in each stage is highlighted to show how over time the "centre of gravity" of each stage will tend to shift up the scale towards higher levels of maturity over time.
3. It is unrealistic to assume that large institutions will find it easy to get past level 3 where the comfort factors are so much higher. The forces of inertia and conservatism will play a part in firms sticking at this level. But once the 3/4 barrier is broken through, the interesting question is whether firms will find it more sustainable and justifiable to move briefly through level 4 and settle rather more happily at level 5. That is an evolving debate that is presently not possible to quantify.

While we have seen in earlier chapters that the development model has some internal momentum driven by an internal logic to answer the questions raised by the previous stage, it is less clear why and how firms may want to become more mature. We find that the most interesting step is the move from level 4 to level 5 and in examining this step we reveal the core mechanisms for change. We also find that the drive to maturity is sufficiently strong to explain most of the development of the stages without the need for any other explanation.

The logic of level 5 is that it is not just fear or the business case that is driving improvements in compliance, but something else. To move from reasons that are essentially self-centered to recognizing "other" is fundamental and is the perfect expression of what we discovered in Chapter 9—the importance of corporate faith.

We can now see that if the level 4–5 boundary is crossed, the role and effectiveness of compliance changes fundamentally. The relationship with the regulator also changes. Most notably, compliance is certain to be embedded, lower-cost, higher quality, professional and successful.

UNCONDITIONALITY

Each step from level to level could be characterized by different dominant motivations, such as:

- Level 1 to 2 = fear of being caught or the business being closed down
- Level 2 to 3 = fear of enforcement or reputational risk, or a desire to do the right thing in compliance terms
- Level 3 to 4 = desire to find a marketing differential or business edge and/or increase compliance effectiveness and flexibility or reduce costs

Each step is important and an evolution, but what is interesting is the process that moves firms from level 4 to level 5.

This is the crunch question: What do firms do of their own volition when no-one is watching? What are their own internalized standards, ways of doing things, expectations, and drivers that move them from maturity level 4 to level 5? This is the ultimate focus for compliance because if a firm will decide for itself that it will operate fairly and honestly, probably beyond the regulatory requirements, then the firm is trustworthy and low-cost to regulate and compliance is ultimately effective.

For compliance and regulation this is the critical determinant—compliance with external standards or internalization and self-driven standards. Compliance will be more successful the more regulatory values and objectives are internalized and surpassed. It is lower cost and more sustainable compliance and regulation. Understanding this difference and enabling a firm to transition to a values-led level is crucial if compliance is to be successful and embedded. And regulators can tell the difference between an organization just playing the game or paying lip service to compliance and one that is values led—although they may not have the necessary tools to measure the difference. The change is from being *dependent* (on the external impulsion of a regulator or public opinion) to being *independent* (and driven by internal values and standards).

What is most interesting is how such a tipping point is reached. It must involve sufficient corporate faith to pursue ethics, pro-compliance culture, good governance, and desirable community outcomes regardless (i.e., unconditionally).

The key dimension of such a values-led state is intent: what the organization wants to do itself, unprompted, what it is, naturally and independently. But is this step conscious or even perceptible at the time? To identify the "crossing of the stream" (or the Rubicon, if you prefer), it is necessary to find evidence of *unconditionality*, that is, the willingness to continue in a course of ethical action even when there may not be a clear advantage to the firm or individual. The ultimate test could be whether such a course of action might lose business or cost money.

Of course, usually a values-led approach will bring the firm business benefits, attract more customers, deliver a marketing edge, and earn even more money, but the business case is not the *starting point*. This is balancing the firm's needs with a wide range of other community interests.

THE UNDERLYING PROCESS

The underlying process that shifts firms from level 4 to level 5 has two components: a high-quality, enabling *Ethical Space* and sufficient corporate faith to impel action. The basic equation is:

$$\text{Ethical Space} \times \text{Corporate Faith} = \text{Corporate Maturity}$$

Let us examine the two components: Ethical Space and corporate faith.

Ethical Space

Drawing on the elements explored in Chapters 4 to 8, we describe an Ethical Space as having five facets, shown in Figure 10.1. The intersection of these five creates an environment that is conducive to ethical consideration and pro-compliance culture.

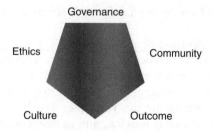

FIGURE 10.1 Five Facets of Ethical Space

These five elements operate together in the same way as the crucible effect described in Chapter 5, although in a more refined, flexible, and all-encompassing way. Perhaps the softer, more enabling character of the Ethical Space could be described as more of a *clearing* with five entrances or sides rather than a crucible pressurizing change. It does not matter how you approach the space or clearing but once inside the five elements are all in contention.

Each facet of the Ethical Space has an essential purpose and all are necessary:

1. Ethics set the basic dimensions (Chapter 4).
2. Culture enables Ethical Spaces to function (Chapter 5).
3. Governance spreads and protects Ethical Spaces throughout the organization (Chapter 6).
4. Outcome gives definition to Ethical Spaces by determining desirable outputs (Chapter 7).
5. Community offers sight of a long-term equilibrium (Chapter 8).

Operating in the Ethical Space requires and draws in all the key processes and concepts described in these chapters:

- Chapter 4: Triangulation—reaching out to multiple points of reference
- Chapter 5: Crucibles—providing robust spaces for change
- Chapter 6: Constructive challenge—raising the quality of decision making
- Chapter 7: Outcome focused—bringing to bear the implications of results
- Chapter 8: Community purpose—locating the organization in a social and sustainable context

All of these work together, and one usually leads on to the next, to create a circle or spiral of learning.

The degree to which the Ethical Space is effective depends upon the:

- Quality of the operation of each element
- Completeness and coherence of the elements working together
- Interrelatedness, complexity, and sophistication
- Pervasiveness of spaces across the organization and at all levels
- Level of commitment to the principles involved, even in times of pressure, when no-one is looking, and in new circumstances where no precedents exist

Corporate Faith

The impulsion to move from a compliance-only approach to an internalised beyond-compliance situation may not be a point-in-time conversion but a gradual transition as the balance of argument, evidence, support, peer-pressure, and external signals builds up. This body of rationale and sentiment is transmitted and developed within the collective structures, power relationships, and values we label as *corporate faith*. Corporate faith is the currency that develops within all the processes described in Chapters 4 to 8, not only drawing them together but also going deeper into each element and the complex that they create together. It is this body of received opinion, habitual practice, and position taking that constitutes the faith on which the firm acts both strategically and day-to-day. This body of beliefs may be accessed consciously, such as through an ethical code, or unconsciously, as part of the firm's normal governance processes, embedded cultural practices, and collective memory—or more commonly a mixture of the two. It is this faith that gives the firm its brand, its roots and heritage, and drives its future direction and ongoing reputation management. It is enshrined or perpetuated in such core documents as the firm's risk framework, risk appetite statement, and management information reporting.

The degree to which corporate faith has developed within the organization is explored in Chapter 9 in terms of its:

- Quality of the operation of each element
- Completeness and coherence, including all of the dimensions
- Interrelatedness, complexity, and sophistication
- Pervasiveness across the organization and through all layers
- Level of commitment to the principles involved, even in times of pressure, when no-one is looking, and in new circumstances where no precedents exist

CORPORATE MATURITY FRAMEWORK

Each component can be considered as a separate axis to create a two-dimensional matrix as in Figure 10.2. Scoring on both axes is subjective (out of 100%) in the same way as risk is scored, with 20 percent nominally allocated to each subcomponent. The scoring of this system will require experience and information sharing, which is not yet available.

We can now locate each of the maturity types across the matrix in Figure 10.2. We can classify firms and sectors across this matrix in the same way as we classify risk. It gives a picture of corporate maturity and compliance performance and embeddedness.

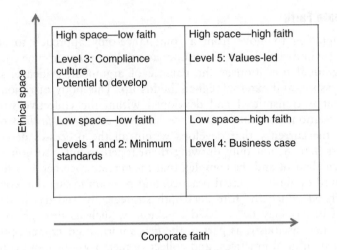

FIGURE 10.2 Maturity Matrix (Ethical Space versus Corporate Faith)

CAVITATION

But the process that draws out and applies that faith in practice in an Ethical Space is simplicity itself. It is at its core an expression of humanity. If you put someone or a collection of people into a space where they have to make up their minds how to act, there is a probability that they will follow their inherent humanity and follow an ethical path. They will do the right thing. All that compliance and regulation can do is to increase the likelihood of that doing the right thing. This is achieved by creating spaces, or clearings, that are conducive to ethical considerations where individuals, firms, and industries sometimes, can step forward and create a human solution. This is an Ethical Space and compliance's contribution is about increasing the likelihood that an ethical outcome will happen; it is not inevitable but likely; it is part of human nature.

We call this *stepping forward into the Ethical Space*, and the consequent flow of value *cavitation*—the name comes from the creation of vacuum lacunae such as at the base of a waterfall that issue forth shockwaves of explosive force-indicating the influential nature of unconditional decisions. These shocks can then create other lacunae in turn and so on.

The moment regulation is started, usually prompted by social progress elsewhere, these Ethical Spaces can be opened up, and good regulations give room for good solutions, which in turn enables compliance and good governance to open up further spaces throughout an organization where positive outcomes can be generated. We described how crucibles operate in Chapter 5. And as individuals and firms have an opportunity to act ethically some will create more opportunities and spaces. It is a flow that can spread anywhere and that has its own momentum. New spaces create more new spaces.

So the underlying process is not amenable to reductionist analysis or a scientific model. This is a continually creative and value- and energy-generating process that arguably reshapes the energy that usually goes to circumventing rules or tick-box compliance to cultural and community change and improvement on many scales. This should give us great hope that compliance systems based on values-led approaches can contribute to producing better outcomes for many.

CONNECTING THE FIVE STAGES OF DEVELOPMENT WITH THE FIVE LEVELS OF MATURITY

The connection is complete in that the development of maturity through cavitation also spreads its effects outwards to create essentially a large-scale Ethical Space and faith across the system that encourages the core parts of the sector, such as regulators and senior compliance staff, to consider short-comings of each stage of development and identify where the development curve should go next. In this sense the whole system moves forward as it deepens; then in moving on to the next stage it needs to deepen and mature once again. The process becomes like a wave motion, moving forward and deepening irresistibly.

CONCLUSION

Charles Darwin's and Adam Smith's processes of natural selection and comparative advantage are those of competition, yet what is described here are ever-widening spirals of cooperation, connection, and co-commitment. As industries and human activities of all sorts become more complex and interdependent the need is to find common linkages, points of connection and common cause. To be in any way manageable, the drive in financial services regulation and compliance is to find ways to agree on shared outcomes, build consensus, and reinforce communities based on mutuality. This requires an overall process of reaching out to find common bases for operation, shared values, ethics, culture, acceptable conduct, and desirable social and economic outcomes held together by open and inclusive governance and agreed articles of corporate faith. These are the processes that produce, sustain, and drive forward the overall progress described in the General Model and the increased maturity set out here.

We have seen in this book a progression through successive stages of sophistication with regulation and compliance adding significant new tools and criteria at each stage. The pace of change has intensified as each new element has been added to reach such a rate and significance that the transformation deserves the title *compliance revolution*. But it is the switch from pure self-interest to a values-led, wider community view that is really revolutionary in nature.

Although the elements described in Chapters 4 to 8 have arrived into regulation sequentially, the real progress has been achieved by working ethics, culture, governance, outcomes, and community together and in an active way. It is the engaging in the development of this compliance landscape that has led to solid progress along the development curve and it is this engagement that delivers overall maturity.

We have seen how compliance and regulation's journey has added new strings to its bow over recent decades. This is necessary if it is to be of strategic value. Compliance needs to understand the current revolution if it is to emerge as a respected and credible profession. The best is yet to come.

So revolution can be justified on two counts. The overall picture is one of evolution but we can say that the pace of change and its fundamental nature explained here amounts to a revolution. But the second justification is more compelling. Each individual act of stepping forward into a space and acting positively is a small revolution, a turning around of the raw basics of 'old compliance'. It is not heroics or courage or a sign of an individual's inward character, experience, or virtue. It is a product of human responses to a wide range of environmental factors that surround us—the ethical considerations, the prevailing culture, the governance framework, a view of outcomes, and community. And it is a collective process. What regulation and compliance provides is space for these countervailing elements to be accessible, to be in contact, to be within the line of sight. The model describes an evolution, the process a revolution.

Index